Little Dipper

Roots of Healing - Tides of Change

by Marlene Denessen, Ph.D.

DREAMCATCHER PUBLISHING
Saint John ● New Brunswick ● Canada

Copyright © 2007 Marlene Denessen, Ph.D.
First Printing, May, 2007

All rights reserved. No part of this publication may be reproduced or transmitted in any form or by any means – electronic or mechanical, including photocopying, recording or any information storage and retrieval system – without written permission from the Publisher, except by a reviewer who wishes to quote brief passages for inclusion in a review.

TITLE: Little Dipper: Roots of Healing - Tides of Change

DreamCatcher Publishing acknowledges the support of the Province of New Brunswick.

ISBN: 978-0-9739234-7-6

BF109.D465A3 2007
615.8'51
C2007-902883-7

Cover Photo: Marlene Denessen

Cover Design: Intuit Design

Editor: B. Christian Crouse

Typesetting: J. Gorman

Printed and Bound in Canada

55 Canterbury St, Suite 8
Saint John, NB, E2L 2C6
Canada
Tel: 506-632-4008
Fax: (506) 632-4009
www.dreamcatcherpublishing.ca

Contents

Acknowledgments 6

Foreword 8

New Brunswick, Canada 10

    Mid-Autumn 13

    Late Winter-Spring 18

    Summer 75

    Autumn 147

Cape Cod, Massachusetts 168

Work Cited 169

Suggested Reading 170

About the Author 171

ACKNOWLEDGMENTS

I would especially like to recognize and thank the people, including family members, who are a part of this story.

Also thanks to Rev. Bill and Patty Thompson, Tony and Caroline Smith, Doug and Lynn Belding, and Jardine and Linda Janes for advice on local accuracy, and the Fredericton breakfast group (Mike Stewart, Phil Vessey, Annabelle Vessey, Ted Roback, Mary O'Keefe Roback, Janice Cook, J.B. Scott, Wendy Scott, and Billy Thorpe) for their cordiality and information about the city.

I owe special acknowledgments to Phillip Lee of Saint Thomas University and to Andrew Titus of the Maritime Writers Workshop at the University of New Brunswick in Fredericton for their guidance and encouragement.

I would like to thank Patty and Rev. Bill Thompson for permission to use photographs of their property, and Torie Laskey for her photos of the cottage on the Nature Conservancy land and the marsh in autumn. Reviews of content by Shirley and Paul Weber, Chuck Hotchkiss, Margaret Eastman, and Rev. Kitsy Winthrop were much appreciated, and thanks to Rita Varley, Librarian for Philadelphia Yearly Meeting, for her assistance with Quaker terminology.

Diane Reynolds and Maryann Zbell, both of Mass. Audubon's Wellfleet Bay Wildlife Sanctuary, were helpful with answers to questions regarding my observations of nature. Robert Prescott, Director of MAWB, provided information about the Sanctuary.

Marv and Nancy Hiles of the Iona Center in Healdsburg, California, provided inspiration through their own published journal material in *The Way Through,* and Tom Tuttle's assistance with communications was most helpful.

Kudos to Betty Ann Lehmann, my dear friend, for being a mentor and a model, and also for being the person I most trusted to read the initial draft of this material.

I am grateful to have been assigned a thoughtful and supportive Editor, Christian Crouse. He made the process both productive and gratifying. Shelley Rogers did a beautiful job with the graphic design of the cover.

And especially – thanks to my Publisher, Elizabeth Margaris, for her encouragement and support, not to mention for being the personification of New Brunswick courtesy, civility, and congeniality.

FOREWORD

I would like to pose a series of questions to those of you who are about to read this book.

Imagine what it might be like to go – alone – to a different country, stay in a cabin in the woods near the sea, and become disengaged from the phone, e-mail, Internet, and even TV for an extended period of time. What might you do? How might you feel? What might happen to you? This is the story of such an experience.

Based upon the journal of my time in New Brunswick, beginning in 2003 and onwards, *Little Dipper* is a book that has begged to be written. Beginning with the publishing itself, which came about through a series of serendipitous events, pieces fell into place. People were home when I called and said yes to my requests. I feel as if there is some purpose to this book that I may never know or understand.

I came north from the States in an openhearted spirit of seeking. It has been over four years since I first unrolled my sleeping bag on the porch, and I have made some observations:

> Deep healing is possible, even of wounds from way back, and even of anger towards God.
>
> Death and rebirth are present all around us, and we are a part of that living stream. To breathe the one breath of the universe in awareness is to be whole.
>
> All moves in the sweep of change. As we pass on, we are roots for new shoots. To surrender to the reality of impermanence is to be at peace.
>
> To allow life to rise up before us is to be free.
>
> We are part of a system that is held in sacred balance – a system of various peoples and of nature. We are stewards of this system. We neglect this stewardship at our own peril.

There are no words to adequately express my love for New Brunswick and my gratitude to the people who have so graciously welcomed me: neighbors, new friends, tradesmen, and fishermen, as well as the folks in the shops, in the offices, and on the phone who have transacted business with uncommon courtesy. You are all a part of the story. You have something very special in New Brunswick. Don't let it slip away.

I have no aspirations to write another book. I am a Psychologist, and I plan to stay with my first profession, at which, at the age of 68, I am still working. But it is nice to think that, when I grow too old to be able to come to New Brunswick, I will be leaving behind this book – and that is very important to me.

NEW BRUNSWICK, CANADA

My car stuffed to the last inch with food, clothing, and furnishings, I drove up the pathway to the tiny cabin. The roof was on and the windows were in, but the single small room was strewn with wood, nails, and sawdust. It was late in the day. I had driven for nine hours, and I had no broom.

I had never slept alone in the woods. Yes, there were trips to campgrounds with my big protective dogs, but this was different. I was a mile in from the tarred road. My only full-time neighbor was a good distance away. There were no curtains for the windows, and it felt downright spooky. I wondered aloud why I had ever done this.

Gathering up courage, I carried in the water, some food, and a sleeping bag. I then dug a slit trench in the woods to use until the outhouse was installed, and prepared a small space on the floor free of debris for my sleeping place. The screen porch would have been the most logical spot, but I was not yet ready for that. It was to be a long night. I finally took a sleeping pill.

During the following four weeks, I tended to the furnishings and the installation of electricity. I dubbed the cabin "Little Dipper" and made a plaque to hang over the door. I acquired property insurance and a postal address, and familiarized myself with the area and with the neighboring city of Saint John.

My friend Betty Ann came from New Mexico to visit. The weather was perfect. Autumn colors were coming in. We spent several days exploring, with long walks on logging roads, bushwhacking through the woods, and stone-picking on the beach. Common time. Priceless treasure. It was nice to have a companion for this first real exploration. It is amazing how fast time can fly when you are in the presence of those who are dear to you.

As the week progressed, I gained a sense of familiarity with the land. Distances seemed to collapse, and the woods began to feel more and more friendly. Betty Ann left, and, as I sat alone in the tiny cabin, well pleased with my choice to come to New Brunswick, I wondered why it had taken me so long to get here....

I was married at the age of eighteen, and had a large family.

Divorced at the age of thirty-two, I returned to school and undertook what turned out to be an intense educational experience. A second marriage ended in divorce, prompting a major move and the re-establishment of my life and my career as a Psychologist. Dad died. Mom came to live with me.

Throughout this time I was changing, becoming increasingly comfortable in my own company and seeking occasions when I might be alone. Clutter became more and more annoying, and I began to simplify.

Then I was given *Beachcombing at Miramar,* a book written by Richard Bode about leaving his nine-to-five city job to live in a beach town, and my intent was clarified.

First came a move to Wellfleet, a small Cape Cod Community, and a downsizing of my business. Another book, *Wherever You Go, There You Are* by Jon Kabat-Zinn, inspired me to begin a meditation practice. My intentions were good, but I kept tripping over life and falling into the familiar pattern of doing, not *being.*

Health problems intervened, and it became physically necessary for me to slow down. I took measures to do this. I went on retreats, my first experiences of extended quiet time. I began to meditate on a more regular basis, but, for the most part, I was still unable to meld my busy life with the stirrings that would not leave me alone.

Little Emma came – and left. My eighth grandchild, she died at the age of four-and-a-half months, just before my sixtieth birthday.

I walked. I grieved. I pondered. I railed against my inability to make things better for my daughter, Emma's mother. The lump in my throat and my clenching esophagus return even as I write this years later.

Struggling with the paradox of Emma's brief life and my own advancing age, I thought of all the things that I wanted to do someday, and began doing them.

I took a grandchild, then sixteen, on a five-week cross-country trip. We traveled by car, slept in a tent, and cooked on a tiny propane-butane stove. The freedom and simplicity were wonderful. Returning to my home, I wondered why my life and surroundings remained so cluttered. The following summer, I took the next grandchild in line, then also sixteen, on a similar trip with a different route.

But there was this other tug. Something. *Something else.*

When I first read *Walden*, Henry David Thoreau's nineteenth-century memoir of his time spent apart in a cabin on Walden Pond in Concord, Massachusetts, I was captivated. It was as if the author had written the book just for me. Five years after Emma died, I came north from the States with the intention of buying or building my Walden.

At other times during my life, a decision to purchase real estate would have taken at least a month, but this time it was different, perhaps because of the way that I went about the search.

A few years ago when I was in Ontario, I came upon an Indian hoop with a legend attached. It seems that many Native people see life as a circle, and believe that, when a decision is necessary, one should not force the issue, but rather proceed as the way opens. I bought the hoop, and carried it with me when I first came to New Brunswick.

I drove through several coastal towns and looked at various properties, but the way did not open until I turned into the dirt pathway and met Darren, the enthusiastic and personable land developer, who returned my call at the very moment when I was leaving the hotel room to return to the States. He showed me a lot that was a short distance from the Fundy shore. I bought it on the spot! The hoop is mounted in a place of honor on the cabin wall.

I hired a local carpenter to build me a fourteen-by-eighteen foot camp, and, for the first time in my life, I experienced what it means to stop. This is a memoir of that experience and of some of the surprises that occurred when I surrendered my agendas and let go – into the present moment.

MID-AUTUMN

Day 1

I have no phone here. There are no diversions from simple living unless I introduce them. The cabin will require little ongoing care. Just a turn of the key to enter or leave. I am ready to learn what the Dipper has to teach.

Today my time has been largely taken up with chores. The place is tiny, and eventually there will be little to do when I arrive except to flip the fuse switch. That will happen soon enough. The activity is good for now. I need to come down slowly.

This afternoon, I took a short walk. The weather was brisk, with a nippy November wind. The air was clean and fresh, and there was virtually no sound. I found deer pellets beside the cabin, fresh deer track in the yard, and bigger track (looked like moose) further back in the woods. I will wear an orange vest whenever I venture off the beaten path, as the very active New Brunswick hunting season has now begun.

Day 2

I awoke this morning to the sound of surf breaking on the rocks. It is strange to have no schedule or agenda. This is new, unfamiliar, and uncomfortable. Is it possible for me to force myself to shut off the noise in my head and stop the incessant activity that I create? Even here, I turn on the radio in order to fill the silence.

Thoreau – on his porch for hours. It sounds great, but how?

Day 3

Today I walked to the sea. The vast Bay of Fundy is the body of water that separates the Maritime Provinces of Nova Scotia and New Brunswick. Folks from these parts are wedded to the ocean, and, at times, she can be a harsh bride.

The shoreline in southern New Brunswick is lined with cliffs, with an occasional break for a rocky beach. I found an unusual stone, with markings resembling a map of the United States overlaid with storm clouds and piercing lines. Then I found another rock, even larger, with delicate, lacey patterns of blue, grey, pink, yellow – all muted and flecked with black. As I turned it in my hand, deposits of mica caught the light. Solid. Heavy. Enduring. A reminder that earth can go on without us.

Walking back to the cabin, I was flooded with the fragrance of balsam fir. The natural world, which often we take for granted, is filled with so many sources of wonder and delight.

Day 4

I spent the day doing errands and finishing up some tasks. I needed a better heater than the one that I brought from home. It is cooler up here than in Wellfleet, and right now it feels like December. I also purchased some odds and ends: a stir-fry pan, a few outdoor tools, and some grass seed to toss around as filler. I have no intention of establishing a lawn. This grass will never see a mower.

A couple of times most every day, I listen to the Canadian Broadcasting Company (CBC), a national radio station that has a full docket of interesting and informative programming. On November 11th, the U.S. celebrates Armistice Day. In Canada, it is referred to as Remembrance Day. There was much on the radio involving the theme of war and how it affects people, including the non-combatants.

Tonight I drove to the pay phone, and, returning up the path, I felt very alone. The lights of my little cabin were the only sign of human habitation. In spite of that, I managed to conjure up the courage to set up a sleeping space on the porch. I must admit that it is very dark at the Dipper in November after 5 P.M., but I wanted to hear the sounds of the night and the rushing of the surf when I awoke in the morning. My anticipation and excitement were stronger than the discomfort of any anxiety.

Day 5

Last night, I slept outside. It was cold, but I was well-covered. I awoke frequently, each time to a different miracle of nature. First, the moon rising over the ledge. Then clouds and stars. Then wind … and the intermittent audible pulsations of the sea. All night long, I was engulfed in the movement and change constantly swirling about me. I felt like the still point in a cyclone of activity. Here, away from distractions, it becomes clear how heedless nature is of us. We are but a mind contemplating it all.

This morning, I had a bit of work done on the place. Before the camp was constructed, a stream that runs through the property was dammed to create a pond. The drop-off on the sides made it dangerous for small children, so I enlisted nearby Coastal Enterprises to make a correction. They sent me Derek, a man who is as skillful with an excavator as an artist is with a paintbrush.

After two loads of fill, the bank now slopes down gradually, and the pond is no more than three feet deep in the center. While the dam was down, I did some mucking about in my high black boots, removing small branches and other debris.

Later in the day, a storm came crashing up from the southeast. It blew in with a fury, buffeting my little house. Tonight, I can actually feel the rumble of the surf through the floorboards as I scrunch down into my sleeping bag. The vibration is almost constant. It is awesome.

Am I really here? Or is this a dream?

Day 6

Yesterday, there was a North Atlantic coastal storm. Today, the surf pounding on the rocks can be felt in every surface of the cabin. This afternoon, as the tide was coming in, toting my disposable camera, I went to Fundy. I was spellbound by the show.

I walked and walked. The rocks along the shore rise precariously high. I carefully picked my way along, mindful of footfalls, moving excitedly from vantage point to vantage point. Like a child at Disneyworld, I was entranced, enchanted. The sea is not unfamiliar to me, and I have spent many long hours walking a beach here, an oceanside trail there. But this was different. The cliffs were sharp and ragged. The ocean, still foaming and spewing, was dark and wild. And I was utterly alone.

As I turned back toward the Dipper, I glimpsed something stark and white against the rock. I stooped to pick up a perfect skull, about the size of the palm of my hand. Big eye sockets. Some molars still intact. Too small for a deer, and too big a snout for an owl. A fox, perhaps. No, the eyes are too large. Never mind. It is not to identify. It is a reminder that time is passing. The past is gone and the future is a dream. Today! Today is the thing.

Soon I will be returning to the States. Having been able to back away a bit, I can see how obsessed I have been by the looming environmental catastrophe, the complacency of many people to the gravity of the situation, and the immersion of the country in a burgeoning culture of consumerism. It all feels quite insane to me, and I do wake at night with concern for the future of my children, and my children's children, and their children yet to come.

Today, in the midst of the storm's aftermath, in the roaring, cascading Fundy waters, a duck of some sort found a pool of quiet sea and sat unperturbed, bobbing up and down, tranquil and easy. Were her children in danger somewhere? Shouldn't she be doing something? Shouldn't she worry?

I cannot change whatever will be by any act of my own, nor will all of my concern have impact upon the course of events. To remain whole I must occasionally step back, at least for a time. In order to live in peace, I must avoid fixating on the parts and, instead, see the picture in its entirety. The foibles of humankind are but one of the parts.

Day 7

Sunrise in November is late, and this morning I was out before dawn. Big black clouds with pink-tinged edges hung heavy in the sky, as the sun tried to make an appearance. The air was moist and sharp in my nostrils. I opened my mouth and drew in long deep draughts. The path before me appeared as a swath cut into dark forest. I imagined myself as Dorothy on the Yellow Brick Road.

This week has been far too short. I feel like a spring uncoiling. Watching ice form on the pond (yes, actually *seeing* it happen), I am able to step out of myself. In spite of my current skepticism regarding religion, I must admit that the circumstances seem to have an air of arrangement about them.

I recently read in the Quaker bulletin that Alice has died. She was in her 90's, and was the first person I met when I attended a Quaker meeting on the Cape. She asked me to tell her about my journey. I told her of the many different churches that I had attended. She responded, "Well, you must be a seeker. All of us here are seekers." I went back again, and will never forget her beautiful smiling face. Yes, I am a seeker. After what? Who knows? No longer after a God, but something much bigger.

Last week, there was a lunar eclipse – the movement of unimaginably huge celestial bodies. My little grandson Kendall said, "The moon is all covered with brown. Come over to my house and you can see it." Yesterday, I found the skull of a small animal. Tonight, as the sun sets, I listen to the chirping of a tiny, solitary bird.

As I settle into sleep, I reflect on the mystery of it all –
the whole of it –
the dance.

LATE-WINTER TO SPRING

Day 1

I left the Cape at 2 A.M. in somewhat of a fleeing mode. Life has been heavy of late. When I find myself awakening in the middle of the night, unrested and unable to go back to sleep, and when this happens more frequently than not, it is time to do something about it.

I love to travel during the early morning hours. There is something very special about driving through sunrise. By 3:30 A.M., I was beyond the Southeast Expressway tunnel, encountering only one other car from the tunnel entrance to Route 93, north of Boston.

Having arrived at Canadian customs at 10:00, I had a nice chat with a border official, stopped at the market in St. Stephen, and felt myself begin to loosen up. I set my watch ahead one hour, and got to the Dipper at 12:30 Atlantic Time. The rest of the day was spent unloading the car and setting up the cabin for an extended stay. Exhausted, I fell into bed at 8 P.M.

Day 2

Last night, I did not sleep well, but at least I managed to stay down until 4 A.M. I am at odds and ends today, unable to meditate, and even distracted from reading. Lots to do. Calls to make. Work to arrange with tradesmen and contractors. I keep moving.

Day 3

For a long time, I have not been happy with how I eat – often reading at the same time, or talking on the phone, or listening to a tape. I would like to taste my food and really enjoy the experience of eating. For breakfast I had cereal, rice milk, and strawberries. Sitting in my favorite spot, quiet and undistracted, I discerned the tastes and textures, and savored every mouthful. Wow! This has promise.

Mr. Deadbolt, the lock man, came in the morning. And then he left. The day was bleak, cold, and raw. The activity had come to an end – and I crashed.

Remembering Dad and thinking about Mom, I wondered how much longer I will have her, and became nostalgic for times gone by, especially my children's early years, and even my own. Last week, I read to Mom from a section in my journal on the days of my childhood. She was enthralled. I could barely hold back the tears. It was very touching.

In any event, I sat, drowning in memories until the day ended, wondering why I came up here to this place . . . so far away ... so unfamiliar.

Day 4

Still unsettled but a little more rested, I brewed some coffee with added vanilla bean. I sat with the steaming cup in my hands, breathing in the aroma, breathing out anxiety and stress. For the first time this week, I really looked out at the woods – chopped and gashed from the logging that has taken place here. But last year's new shoots are everywhere. Earth endures.

Preparing for a long walk on rough trails, I fashioned a safety package. Winding an ace bandage around the top of my long walking stick, I anchored it with pins and covered it with duct tape to keep it dry. It could come in handy, should I need to wrap a sprain or splint a more serious injury.

When I arrived on Wednesday, the pathway was covered with deer tracks. Darren verifies that there are moose here, and the lock man said that there are bear. People tell me that bear are timid and that they will avoid people who make loud noises. I always carry a police whistle around my neck when I walk in the woods.

As the day winds down, I return to the Dipper. Here, tucked in the woods, I neither see nor hear human activity. The silence and solitude are beginning to become friendly and comfortable. I am a little disappointed that I am unable to sleep on the porch. The earth is still frozen, and it sends up bone-chilling cold and dampness. It will be nice, however, to anticipate a warm night – and maybe even peepers – as spring thaw begins.

Day 5

Up at 6 A.M., I turned on the radio to see if Canada had set its clocks ahead, and the first thing that I heard was a group of little children singing "Good Morning to You." That sure took me back. When I was a child, we began every school day with that song.

Today is Sunday and my day in the city. I was dressed in my best and out the door by 8:30 A.M., looking for the Unitarians in Saint John. After a brief search, I found the Carleton Community Center, a big old brick building that has a door of bright yellow with tree-like designs – a good sign of what goes on within.

It was another in a series of drizzly days, and the bleakness once more gave rise to the thought: "Marlene, have you lost your mind? Alone, way up here?" However, I am learning to trust my instincts and take the next step. I pulled my car up to the curb and waited, and along came a pleasant man. He invited me to join the UU gathering. The interior of the place is beautiful. Large rooms. High ceilings and 1940's decor. I was transported back in time over fifty years. It reminded me of many of the studios where I would go as a little girl with my father when he was teaching music. Those buildings are now all gone.

This was Singing Sunday. About seven of us gathered around an upright piano that my grandparents would recognize. We sang some songs and chatted. The people were congenial and welcoming. I will return.

I then went uptown to the Aquatic Center for a relaxing afternoon. This huge complex, composed of pools and a health club, has been the site of the Canada Games and is a health promoting focal point for this major New Brunswick city. Today it was full of children of all sizes and ages. There were several learn-to-swim classes going on simultaneously. Parents waiting for their children and folks in the sauna, hot tub, and steam room seemed to know one another. I felt a strong sense of community.

I stopped at the payphone in order to check in at the office. A client is in crisis. Many people have difficult lives.

My own life has not been easy, but I have an observation. It took the accumulation of years and a certain amount of real trouble to wear away the veneer of entitlement and put an end to the illusion that life is meant to be fair. Even the rocks on this armored coast lose ground.

I must admit that approaching sixty was difficult. There was no longer any doubt: my physical body was changing. In a culture of idealization of all things young and beautiful, I was growing old. And what was I to make of that? What was I to do? What a strange question when there is nothing to be done. Nothing at all. It took me a while to accept the reality of the downhill slide. I now experience a new dimension of freedom. Such paradox – to surrender into freedom.

My sixties have been unequivocally the best years of all. Utter defeat! I'm old and that's OK. The great challenge is to accept your life as if you had planned it that way.

Tonight, for the first time since I arrived, I meditated peacefully and assembled yarn and knitting materials for a project for New Baby – coming soon.

Day 6

I experienced some middle-of-the-night sleeplessness, with thoughts of my children and situations in their lives, but eventually I drifted off. I arose at 8 A.M. and looked out of my window at a living mural – rural New Brunswick in the snow! Four inches or so covered everything, hanging in the pointed firs, setting off the sculpture of the ledges. A skin of ice on the pond struggled to stay firm as the temperature hovered near freezing.

Attempting meditation, I fought my racing mind until I remembered not to fight but instead to simply allow the thoughts to pass through, touching them lightly and coming back to the breath. I eventually surrendered to the old faithful method of counting breaths . . . one to ten . . . one to ten . . .

My spirituality, which once was so formal and organized, has now been reduced to absolute simplicity. I recall teachings from one of my favorite sources of wisdom, *The Tao Te Ching*. The Tao can neither be named nor described. It is the path to understanding. It is all that is, and it is nothing at all.

Bundled up and toting my camera and walking stick, I set off for a saunter in this winter wonderland. Torie came driving up the path with her little girl and her Golden Retriever. They were visiting their land for a winter picnic. At the main road, I met Nell on her way to work. She is living temporarily in the only year-round house in the area.

I walked for a long while. The oceanfront was gorgeous in the snow. I ventured onto a side trail that, I believe, is frequented by moose. Sure enough – moose tracks. My adrenaline surged.

I continued on. I wanted to get to the white cliffs, a place with a million dollar view out over the pointed firs to the sea. Was it ever worth it! And the silence – there is something so very special about a snow silence.

By now my stomach was calling, and I decided to have a treat. I cooked porridge – the old-fashioned kind that you stand over and stir for ten minutes – laced with pine nuts, currants and sunflower seeds, and drowned in rice milk. I am learning to discover when I am satisfied with what I have eaten but not necessarily full, and especially not stuffed. I also am not eating just because it is mealtime, or because the food happens to be there, or because I am anxious about something and food helps to calm my anxiety. I am waiting until I actually feel hungry. Novel idea.

Thoughts of my children surface. It is my hope that they understand the intent and spirit of my coming here, and that they do not feel abandoned in some way when I leave for extended periods of time. Betty Ann and I frequently discuss our involvements with our families. She also goes on long and distant journeys, having little contact with her children while she is away. She refers to it as practice, for us when we have to make our final exit, and for our children when they won't have us anymore.

The day flies by. Earlier the snow turned to rain, and now it is back to snow again. Another walk? Yes! The wind is coming up and is whistling in the wires. Water from melting snow is flowing out of cracks and crevices everywhere, creating little rivulets and a symphony of gurgles and splashes.

Two foghorns converse with each other. It is dead low tide and the ocean smell, combined with the fragrance of spruce, is fantastic. All of my senses are alive! All bundled up, cold weather walks makes me feel so whole and well.

This evening, the Dipper looks like a mountain climber's hut in the White Mountains of New Hampshire on a rainy day, with wet clothes hanging everywhere. Time for meditation, a crossword or two, and bed.

Day 7

It was another restless night. I awoke somewhere mid-way through, pondering some familial difficulties. Once I begin to do this, I cannot get back to sleep. Very few meaningful and useful solutions emerge when I am in this state.

On the Cape, I have occasionally been attending Quaker meetings, albeit in an irregular manner. The Quakers have a silent gathering for worship with no minister, no creed, and no dogma. They believe that there is "that of God" in everyone and that each of us has the capacity to be in some form of contact with this higher power. It is church in progress, as the politics of Quakerism changes with the discernment of the people.

Sometimes during the meeting, individuals have a calling to speak, often accompanied by a physical quaking of sorts. This is really true. It has happened to me. Our Yarmouth Friends Group tends to be quiet, and testimony is the exception rather than the rule. For me, this is comfortable. The silence is balm for the soul.

Most of the Quakers in New Brunswick are in the Fredericton area, about ninety minutes from the Dipper. There is a little group in St. Andrews, but that is also far away. In any event, Quakerism calls me back. We'll see where it goes.

Time to get bundled up and out into the weather. Heading for Fundy, I walk through a grove of fir trees, their bows heavy with snow.

The sea is now dead flat. Only the subtle shift in level associated with the incoming tide makes any discernable sound. The sky and water are of identical hue – matte silver-grey. Nothing moves as snowflakes fall around me. I drink in the delicious aloneness of this day, this place, this moment in time.

Back in the cabin, I sit with a cup of tea as the weather swirls about. Sleet turns to hail. Hail turns to flurries. I sit.

I reflect.

I watch the snowflakes. Each one unique, they are intricately beautiful. Like us, they have short lives. My reflection peers back at me from the window. Old. I have grown old. Like the snowflakes, we are all blown about and tossed asunder. There – one lands on the deck. And it is gone.

I settle into mid-afternoon meditation. I am finding it helpful, when my mind drifts off, to collect myself with the question, "What is happening now?" This little teaching was given about four years ago at a Zen learning day, but I never before understood it experientially. Whether walking, sitting, or lying down, something is always happening besides the noise in my head. Perhaps the sun is caressing the side of my face, or there is the song of a bird, or even the motor of the refrigerator. All of these things happen in the present moment. The noise in my head is almost always linked with something from the past or some projection into the future. Now is when life is lived. The past and the future have only to do with the events and situations of my life.

Another Zen teaching has to do with impermanence. Many of us take the earth and its environment for granted. Perhaps this is because we take our own importance and ourselves so seriously. We need to remember that we are only here for a little while, and that others will follow. Our individual lives are brief, but the life of the planet goes on. In Native culture, consideration was given to the seventh generation to come.

As snow falls in tiny balls that bounce on the deck, shifting breezes blow it back against the cabin. *Ping-ping. Rat-a-tat.* It looks like bits of Styrofoam. The deck becomes white with it.

And then – what a treat! Across the meadow and into the yard bounds a snowshoe hare. I have never seen one before. Almost as large as a cat, its rangy movements put me in mind of a kangaroo. Still mostly white, it is nicely camouflaged in the snow. Small flecks of brown give it a tweedy look.

I think of Emma. Right after she died, on my first long walk after I returned to Wellfleet, I encountered a rabbit. I was saddened by the thought that she would never see one. I told her that I would take her with me and show her the bunnies through my eyes. I sure hope that this one stays around.

See the bunny, Emma?

Sitting for a bit, I thought about prayer. I find myself to be at a loss for words as to how to explain how I pray. I also struggle to articulate a conceptualization of a higher power. These reflections from the UU literature come close:

"God is . . . the acknowledgment of the mystery . . ."
"I pray because alone I am not enough, and also, when
I pray, I acknowledge that God is not me . . . "

Ask me if I think that a higher power arranges things and that every hair on my head is numbered, and I would say no. But ask me if I trust that I am being guided in some particular direction, that is a different story. Ask me if I believe that prayer is effective in getting us what we want. Again, no. Do I pray? Yes. Am I confused? Sure. Has something been lost? You bet. All the many words have sunk like pearls in syrup, and I sit – face on with the mystery of it all.

I go to the winter beach at full high tide. The waves wash the shore. As they recede, they pull little pebbles down the incline. How I love the rushing sound that this creates. I pause for a time and listen to the rustling of the branches, the *click-clack* of the stiff winter birch, and the intermittent, luxuriant quiet.

Day 8

Finally! I had a normal sleep and awakened rested and refreshed. Lolling in my sleeping bag, it occurs to me that I have nowhere to go and nothing to do. No lists. No plans. Such luxury. Bundled in my chair with aromatic steam rising from my coffee, all's right with the world.

Days have been mostly overcast, with occasional light drizzle or flurries – damp and cold by most standards, but I really don't mind this weather. If I am chilly, I just do a few vigorous step-ups before I begin my walk. Also, the terrain here is uneven and hilly, and this keeps my blood pumping and my body warm.

The sea, the absence of human sound, the pointed firs and the rugged cliffs lend to feelings of tranquility that I cannot put into words. I felt like this in Wellfleet at first. I can still get a sense of it now and then, especially on a stormy day when there is no one around, or when the smell of the sea is right, or when the seagulls squawk just so. The problem is that I brought my life to Wellfleet. That will not happen here.

Walking the cross ridge trail, I am stopped dead in my tracks by a musky animal smell – rank and heavy. Someone told me that the presence of bears is announced by their odor. I pulled out my whistle and stood still. Nothing stirred. I turned around and headed back. The ridge road will have to wait until another day.

It's time to do a little housework. Sweep up. Empty the compost and wash the chamber pot. Basic tasks for basic needs.

~

I go to the pay phone to make some calls. There's trouble at home! I drive to Dipper Harbour, a nearby fishing village, park the car by the dock, and sit. In a three-minute phone call, I am plunged backward. They are constructing a new pier. I sit and watch. I sit some more.

I go back to the cabin and write a letter. Now, the silence is deafening and the solitude is unfriendly. I feel agitated and sad. I rewrite the letter. I eat compulsively and make plans for tomorrow. I will keep busy for a day, and then maybe I can come back down.

I rewrite the letter again. Should I put it in the mail? Maybe I will buy a card in which to send it. I bring a book-on-tape into the cabin. Listening to audiotapes is a sure-fire way to take my mind off a problem. It is 9:45. Sleep is a fantasy tonight. I put on the tape and zip myself into my sleeping bag. I want to cry. I take a sleeping pill.

Day 9

I awaken this morning with a question: Over the years that I have been an adult, have my parents told me when they thought that I was headed in a wrong direction? Yes, they have. They did not incessantly hammer me with advice. They simply told me what they thought and loved me. I will rewrite the letter and send it in a card.

The sun is out and I am up at 8:30. The snow is almost gone. I brew a pot of green tea and watch the birds. The tiny teacup in my hands is warm. The steam is lightly aromatic with pear. The tea slides down and warms me from the inside out.

~

I went into the city, and found a perfect card for the letter. After buying a souvenir for Mom, I struck out on a self-guided walk along the Loyalist Trail. The city of Saint John was the first settlement in the Province. The people who originally came here emigrated from the United States. They were loyal to the Crown and did not wish to take part in the Revolutionary War.

Along the route were a series of beautiful old buildings – churches, storefront businesses, and private homes. There was a disastrous fire here in the 1870's that destroyed a major part of the city. Most of the buildings date from that time. I visited the Court House, an old building in its own right with an elegant white marble spiral staircase. It is still used for judicial proceedings.

On two separate occasions, folks noticed that I was fumbling with a map and asked me if I could use some assistance. A man showed me the building in which his father and grandfather practiced law, and then pointed out his own law office.

I swung back around the harbor. Many boats were in – a Norwegian cruise ship, a massive container ship, and various smaller vessels. There is much industry. Saint John is a muscled city.

Stopping at City Market, a wonderful old-fashioned shopping place with all kinds of goodies and produce, I purchased some fresh-squeezed orange-strawberry juice and sat for a spell to people-watch. The old-faithful escape into *busy-ness* works again.

Day 10

Last night, I slept in my sleeping bag with the window open to the clean night air. The day dawned with bright sunshine and a crystal clear sky. Little snowbirds twittered as they foraged in the corn that I had provided. Starting the day with scrambled eggs and cantaloupe, hot water and lemon – and silence – I am coming down for a second landing.

As I sat in the bright afternoon sun on the stoop, I pondered how I came by this love of the outdoors. Certainly not from either of my parents. Perhaps from my father's mother's forebears: they lived in the cold north woods of Wisconsin. My father told me that they would hear the wolves howling at night. Or, even more likely, from my mother's father's family. I recently found out that they were French, most probably from Quebec. Many French Canadians were woodsmen. I wish that I knew more about my ancestors. It occurs to me that, as we before them, our progeny are as arrows shaped by forces beyond knowledge and control, and shot into the new day.

It was a perfect afternoon for outside work, so I trimmed some brush in order to make a trail. Because of a chronic condition, I have to be careful of my back, but I can still do a few small tasks now and then. The trail jigs and jags around stumps and rocks, and curves back on itself in a switchback. It terminates at the top of a hill. The panorama is gorgeous.

Later, I stopped at the payphone to check in back home. Tom says that his condition is deteriorating and that he is going to start chemotherapy earlier than originally planned. Dear Tom. He is such a good friend. And Karen. Such a special woman. She is experiencing pain from the double mastectomy that she had last week, but she is up and about and enjoying visits from people who care about her.

It is Holy Week. This season is so different for me now. A friend from the States has been to see *The Passion of the Christ* two times. He said that he cried his way through it, and that it dramatized for him just how much Jesus suffered for us.

When he suggested that I should see it, I responded that I had seen enough innocent suffering in the Pediatric Intensive Care Unit of the children's hospital to last the rest of my life. Tiny babies anchored to life by beeping machines and entanglements of gurgling tubes. Parents – desperate parents – sitting helplessly. My daughter, pumping milk from her breasts – it is all that she can do. Nursery songs in the background: "London Bridge is Falling Down." Yes. I can see that it is. It surely is.

That is how it was. And that is enough for any Holy Week for me.

~

Meditation is difficult today. My mind is all over the map. I breathe into the thoughts again and again, letting go with the out-breath. Let go. Let go. Let go.

Down to a sweater and light jacket, I leave for a long, slow walk on paths through the woods by brooks and streams, encompassed about by mist. Foghorns converse intermittently, low and muffled. Ethereal ... like this day – this place.

I walk. I remember.

Day 11

I awoke this morning at 6:45 and slipped into deep meditation ... breathing in ... breathing out ... There is nothing to accomplish in this time when I sit. Just returning to the breath when my mind wanders off is entirely enough ... breathing in ... breathing out ... letting thoughts fade into emptiness at the end of each exhalation.

It turned out to be a beautiful early-spring day. I took off a layer of clothes including my long underwear, washed my hair, and got really clean. Living without running water challenges me to find novel methods to wash dishes and to bathe. This entire adventure has reinforced my sense of self-reliance. What a wonderful feeling for a sixty-five year old woman. There is a sentence stem that is often used in Psychological testing: "The most important thing that I know is ..." I don't have to ponder my response for long. The most important thing that I know is ... that I can make my way in the world.

Sitting on the stoop, I dried my hair in the sun and luxuriated in the taste and texture of a Bosque pear. As I turned to go inside, I noticed that something was billowing out from a stand of spruce. It looked like smoke at first glance, but then it was everywhere. It was fog rolling through the trees from the sea, crawling along the road.

Nothing to do. Just sit. Just watch.

Day 12

Today, I was up at 7 A.M and off to spend Easter with the UUs. As I was a little early, I explored the adjoining neighborhood. There are many working-class people here, residing mostly in flats, with a smattering of single homes. I stopped at a Tim Hortons for coffee. Folks were friendly, volunteering helpful information about Saint John and its environs, and suggesting things that I might do the next time that I go into the city.

The service was typically Unitarian, a beautifully orchestrated non-denominational celebration of gratitude, spring, and new beginnings. UU stands for Unitarian Universalist. The Unitarian Universalist Church is open and affirming. All forms of spirituality are respected. UUs honor the Truth in all religions.

Some of the folks, upon learning that I attend Friends meetings back in the States, offered to locate the New Brunswick Quakers for me. I am beginning to really appreciate the unpretentious, substantial, and solid feel to the Carleton Community Center, not unlike the people I am meeting inside.

Back at the Dipper on my afternoon walk, I found a pathway that turned me back. Torie told me about this trail, which passes across her property and into a deep and dark wood, eventually leading to a rocky beach. There was a narrow path that showed little sign of current usage. There had been no logging, but there were lots of fallen trees with huge clods of disturbed soil around their exposed roots. Outside of little patches of sunshine, there was a foreboding air about the place.

A massive tree had fallen across the trail. It had all kinds of clefts and cubbies where little animals like porcupines and skunks might live. In other places where I have walked, I have been alone, but I could see out of the forest around me, and I could be seen. The feeling of being hidden away on a path that was virtually never used did not sit well. I will come back, but with a companion.

Day 13

This was a peopled day. Torie was back, and this time with both of her little girls, Alex and Lucinda. Peter, the Warden, dropped in. He is the husband of Shirley, the pleasant and helpful office manager at Coastal Enterprises. Peter described the area as a place where folks take care of one another. He told me that I am very safe here.

I did some more light trail work. Just on my four-acre plot there are all kinds of mini-ecosystems. A stream fed pond. Lichen. Pools of stagnant water. Soft, moist, and moldy decaying wood – loose and crumbly to the touch. Last year's ferns, dried to fragile brown skeletons. Field grass and raspberry bushes. Hundreds upon hundreds of little birch trees, crowding into each other. Boulders and logs for the children to climb on, and, best of all, a dark, deep, moss-covered grove. I can visualize my grandchildren, Alyssa, Derrick and Mark, Kendall, Sydney and New Baby, being make-believe afraid of this perfect setting for the "Teddy Bears' Picnic."

I made a choice many years ago. I chose my grandchildren as the primary focus of my free time. This was a conscious decision. When I would like to have a date, I pick up the phone and arrange for a movie, a dinner, a special event, a weekend of fun on the Cape, or a trip. The kids and I have been so good for each other. This certainly was one of the best decisions that I have ever made.

Sometimes, when I am with one of my grandkids, I have a lapse from the activity at hand and an inventory of the times we have shared rolls out like a scroll before me. A sweetness rises in my throat. I catch my breath in recognition of the magnitude of the sum of all these special moments and the poignancy of passage.

Today, I savored lunch. Salad with a hard-boiled egg, eaten mindfully and ever so slowly, is a gourmet meal. A piece of spinach with a touch of olive oil. Yum! The taste of a radish explodes in my mouth. The flavor of fresh cucumber is delicate, even a little sweet, and its composition is almost all liquid. Thoroughly chewed, there is virtually nothing left.

~

The Nature Conservancy owns a large piece of land nearby. This class act organization seeks to preserve open space all over the world. The New Brunswick parcel contains some of the most beautiful Fundy-front property.

I set out to locate the Nature Conservancy land, and came upon an abandoned tiny house poised on the tip of a cove. Circling the house and looking in the windows, I wondered about the people who had lived there.

Laying down in an adjoining soft mossy field and watching the clouds pass, I immersed myself in the sounds of wind, water, and even a loon. Lovely.

For supper, I made a concoction of brown rice, fresh cauliflower, broccoli, carrots, spinach, and sunflower seeds, topped with minced clams and clam juice. Passing by satisfied, I slid beyond full, and came to a roaring stop at stuffed. So much for slow, reflective, and meditative eating.

Meal preparation has become virtually effortless. I have surrendered to the modern technology of a microwave. Every two weeks or so, I make a huge pot of soup on the single burner hot plate and portion it into glass jars. I turn the tiny refrigerator up to max and use it as a freezer, popping a single serving into the micro and having hot, full-bodied and healthy homemade soup in a matter of minutes. I buy as much organic food as I can. It feels wonderful to have the time to shop and cook in a leisurely fashion.

Day 14

I stay in bed until 10:15 A.M., unheard of in my lifetime since my teenage years. It is raining today. Watching the raindrops falling on the pond is an hypnotic experience. Thousands of continuously expanding circles burst against the mosaic of the pond bottom, now composed of vivid green algae, dead and rotting leaves, and brown sod.

Both the Fire Chief and the Warden have suggested that I have a phone so that, in the case of a problem at the nuclear plant nearby, I can be alerted and advised as to the best exit route. New Brunswick provides all people within a fixed radius of the nuclear power facility with a device that attaches to the telephone and sounds loudly should an emergency arise. Potassium Iodide pills, to be used in such a situation, are delivered to every home and replaced with a new supply when their date of expiration is reached.

I can't imagine introducing a phone to this place. My colleague, Paul, provides professional coverage for me, and, in order for family members to reach me in the case of an emergency, I have left local contact numbers. I call my mother every other day from the pay phone, which is three miles away. It is beyond me how people can tolerate, via cell phone, being immediately available to anyone at any time all the time.

Finally my jaw has relaxed, the tightness in my chest has loosened, and my racing mind has quieted. I sit by my radiator in the little cubby that I have created by walling off a small portion of the room with insulated curtains so as to preserve heat. I write. I read. I knit.

A foghorn drones in the distance. This is one of those dark early-spring days when I feel the need to move in order to get the blood pumping.

~

On a long walk, I passed through a village and came upon a big, shaggy black dog standing ahead of me – face on. His ears were up and he looked friendly. I did my "nice puppy" routine, and he came trotting over. We exchanged greetings, and I moved on. He followed.

A short distance down the road, the dog disappeared into a yard. I heard some doggie noises, and he re-emerged with a big brown companion. They frolicked together for a moment, and then went off into the woods with the black dog leading.

Memories flooded back of our beloved Underdog, a black Labrador Retriever, and her friend Casey, a Springer Spaniel. Every morning Casey would arrive at our back door and summon Underdog. After wagging hellos to one another, off they would go into the woods to hunt in team fashion. On one occasion, I watched them corner a woodchuck. Best friends running free. I'm glad that there are still places like 1970's Seekonk, Massachusetts.

After lunch, I bushwhacked out to my back property line. Slash from the logging is still visible, but within a couple of years it will have given itself completely over to the land. Death is woven into the fabric of the landscape. A clinging on for a season, and then a letting go. I pondered impermanence and the fact that I – and even the Dipper – are just passing through. Because my time on earth is limited, the time that I have is all the more precious.

Soon new life will be bursting forth everywhere. The old and the new will blend into a unity. Death to life. In old roots there is a stirring of new shoots.

Since Emma, it has become increasingly comfortable for me to live in the mystery of all of this. I don't need to know what happens next. Life turns on its own, and I will turn with it. That's all.

That's all.

Day 15

Today I took a long walk along wet wooded paths, sinking in mud to my ankles. Meandering about, I was caught up short by some little yellow flowers growing out of the crushed rock underpinning of a logging road – beautiful shining faces looking south at the sun. I found a good spot and lay down amongst them, giving myself over to the brilliant sunshine and the wrap-around sound of the wind rustling last year's tall dry grass.

Heading back, I stopped at a well-kept cemetery peopled mostly by Thompsons, a very common name in these parts. I came upon the grave of a little girl who was born in 1959 and died in 1961. I then found a tombstone from the 1930's with the names of three siblings on it, all of whom died within the first few days of life. How difficult it must have been for the folks who had to live with the impact of these tragedies.

As I turned to go, I noticed a movement behind one of the stones. I stood very still and waited. It was a porcupine. He paused for a moment, and then lumbered across the grass to a tree, which he slowly climbed to the topmost branches. There he clung, swaying to and fro, looking down on me. I have been told that wild animals live a parallel and equal life, and that we can observe it but we cannot enter it. I can tell you that, for a moment today, that porcupine and I occupied the same mental space.

Day 16

I roll out of bed at 8 A.M. with the full day ahead, nothing to do, and not a skeleton of a plan. It's raining and it's cold, but who cares? I don't even know what day of the week it is.

The April rain has filled the pond to the brim. Water is pouring in from the brook, creating a symphony of gurgles and babbles. The water is dark and heavy with the minerals that are plentiful in this rocky place. The pond is fed by a stream that comes out of the ground at the boundary of my property. By last August, small insects and frogs had moved in, some pond grass had begun to grow close to the shore, and algae had started to form.

The pond is a reflection of what is happening around it. On some days, it is still, a mirror for the surrounding rocks. At other times, it is in constant motion, stirred by the wind and pelted by the rain. At all times, it waits upon the action of elements other than itself. As the rain continues and the brook becomes a tiny waterfall, little ships of white foam take shape and drift like an armada toward the dam.

A respite at the Dipper is a major break in the usual pattern of life. Because of this, it provides opportunities for novelty, and presents new possibilities for a healthy life style. I have already made many positive changes over the past decade, especially involving exercise and diet. I am attempting meditation and am convinced of the positive impact of this practice, but when I am back on the Cape and the wheel of life gets rolling, I surrender to the motion, and time for meditation is one of the first things to go. Usually, a dark Wellfleet weekend gets me back on track.

I recently heard of some new research. It has been reported that stress does not affect health in a negative way as long as it is not prolonged and unremitting. The researchers advise that occasional stress, followed by respite and renewal, is actually strengthening. It is the availability and quality of stress relief that is important.

The well drillers have arrived! And with them, the snow. In the path they come with a thirty-ton rig. It is as big as the cabin. Their back-up truck broke a drive shaft on the way in and is stuck. They are making do, drawing water from the pond and lugging heavy pipes and logs. I provide fruit, rice cakes and peanut butter, and tea. Real men up here actually drink tea. After several hours of drilling, no water is at hand.

Day 17

I opened the door this morning to blowing snow, a chorus of foghorns, and a yard full of well-drilling machinery. The well was a success, but not a gusher. Over two hundred feet down, virtually all rock ledge, the drill hit water. After finishing up, Jim and Jim moved on to the job of changing the drive shaft. Sliding under the truck in the snow and on the rocks, they hammered away, and, after a substantial period of time, they got the vehicle up and running again.

A pump was installed and a hose spigot attached. Now I have electricity and outdoor plumbing. The place is becoming less and less like Walden.

The late day is cast in shades of lavender. The pond is especially beautiful tonight, the blackness of the water walled about by the white and sepia of the landscape. There is a feeling in the air of endings and new beginnings. The closed-in weather of winter that calls forth primitive remembrances of hibernation will soon be over for another year.

The magic of springtime is about to burst upon us. I will never cease to be amazed by the mysteries of nature. For example, how does a tree produce a leaf, expelling it from a tiny branch? The miracle of a brain and thought – how does it ever happen? The yearly journey of the Monarch Butterfly to a single gathering place in Mexico – it boggles my mind to imagine the instinct and drive of these fragile creatures, and the rigors of their incredible journey. And how about fire? Not to mention healing? I suspect that all of this is easily explained by evolutionary and biological science. But what about joy? What about wonder?

In pondering the mysteries of life, Buddhists often use *koans*, which essentially are unsolvable puzzles. For example: "What was your original face? How did you look before your grandmother was born?"

Tonight, I did an inside walking meditation. I find that this is best done without shoes, so as to feel through my feet the surface on which I walk. Step . . . Step . . . Pressure on the right foot, slowly shifting to the left . . . Step . . . Step . . . . The room darkens gradually. Pacing the perimeter of the tiny cabin by candlelight, I have the impression that the Dipper is the most beautiful dwelling in the entire world.

~

It snowed off-and-on all day and cleared toward nightfall. I spent the rest of the evening rediscovering the joy of knitting. There is an excitement in planning a creation for someone I love and a sense of satisfaction in watching it progress. Once I settle in, it takes on a meditative quality. The needles and the yarn. The pattern and the smooth methodical movement . . . Back and forth . . . Back and forth . . . .

I finished New Baby's strawberry hat. Having completed a violet boa for Mommy Amy, I will now start a pumpkin head for big sister Sydney.

Supper was scrumptious! Home-fried potatoes, butternut squash, and scrambled eggs. I finished the day listening to a live concert carried by the radio, featuring pipes, fiddles, accordions, flutes, whistles, trumpets, percussion, and even singing in Gaelic. The music filled the cabin with full-bodied ethnic sound.

Day 18

After another restful night, I awoke this morning to the rumblings of what I thought was the wind, shaking the house and roaring like a freight train. I remembered the sound – a heavy, constant, low whine – from a time spent back in the States with my mother, evacuated to the high school during Hurricane Bob. It was dark. I meditated prone, as I often do in the morning.

My thoughts once again drifted home to my other life, but now something was different. I felt no tightening in my chest, and my jaw remained slack. I also experienced a sense of clarity unavailable in the midst of turmoil.

I am learning some things. I do not need to feel guilty that I cannot be everything to all people all of the time. If I am to function in a healthy way for the many folks with whom I am closest and all the others with whom I have a helping relationship, I must take care of myself. To the outward world, I am calm and stable, steady and rational. Inside, especially when the people I love are hurting, I am just like everyone else – aching and raw.

So the long and short of it is that I need to have a plan. Choices do exist, and I am ultimately in charge of my own life. When I am back in Wellfleet, I need a buffer time around my sleep – a time of quiet in the evening in order to shut down and again in the morning in order to move slowly into the day. To do this I need to control my phone. That means no calls between 7:30 P.M. and 8:00 A.M. There are very few problems that are of such great magnitude that they cannot wait for a few hours, and I will be in better condition to help, having had adequate mental rest.

I also need to learn to say no without feeling guilty. I am aging. It is the simple truth that I can no longer do what I did in my fifties if I wish to stay well. There is an old Zen saying: "If you point your car south when you want to go north, how will you arrive?"

I arise at 8 A.M. to a cold and dreary day and a developing coastal storm, different from that on the Cape. The shoreline here faces south into the sea, into the storms of the open Atlantic. I poke my head out of the door to discover that the sound that I had heard was not the wind. It was the ocean. The constant rumble is coupled with intermittent muffled thuds. I can feel them in the cabin floor under my feet. Surf. Big breaking surf. I must go!

Layers of clothes later, I embark with my walking stick and camera. The ice on the pond has completely melted. The rain is so fine that it is as if millions of tiny specks of sand are breaking the surface of the water.

I walk to the ocean. Facing into the storm, the wind and spray take my breath away. The sea is covered with white spew and foam. I walk the paths over the cliffs and along the shore. On days like this, all exposed to the weather, the fir trees emit an especially sharp and sweet fragrance. I draw it in deeply. I bathe in the fullness of this Fundy fury. Of all the possible highs in life, this wins hands down for me.

~

On the way back to the Dipper in the rain, I met Tom and Lyndsay, here from the States with their daughter Stephanie. Later in the day, Patty, a neighbor and the wife of Preacher Bill, stopped to visit and invited me to her home tomorrow night for a turkey dinner. Patty and Bill have a lovely farm with a classic gabled Canadian home.

Day 19

About midway through the night, I awoke to a sky full of stars and the sound of a bell buoy. Later still, there was the far-off call of a loon. At early dawn, everything was cast in shades of grey. The trees were silhouetted against the pond in stark relief. At about 7:15, I was roused to the new season by the serenade of a song sparrow. The surf is pounding against the rocks this morning, and the bell buoy is sounding constantly. There is a pulse here . . . beating . . . beating . . . .

I am aware that I am becoming subject to occasional unbidden feelings of well-being. Real physical feelings. Is this serenity? Peace? Whatever it is, I'll take it!

~

Today, I joined the Quakers in St. Andrews. They meet on the second floor of the Sunbury Shores Arts and Nature Center on the main street of town. The room is large, bright, and elegantly unmodernized, as is the case in most Quaker gathering places. The Quaker Community in St. Andrews is small. Julie, Lee-Ann, and Larry are regulars, and a smattering of others attend more infrequently. Like Quakers everywhere, they are simple-living and solid. Like the UUs, they give me an open-arms welcome.

I came back to a turkey dinner at Patty and Bill's. Their son

Herb and his friend Michelle were present, as were Nell, Tom, Lyndsay, and Stephanie. The food was wonderful, as was the Maritime hospitality.

I drove home at about 9 P.M. on this gorgeous early-spring night. The first scent of spring soil, warming after the passing of the last snow, was lifted in the air. The sky, not totally darkened, was metallic grey laced with wispy black clouds. One lone star shone, and peepers began to sing as I entered my yard.

I stood, captivated and lost in the spell of it. The fresh and clean smell of earth renewed. The movement of day into night. And I am a part of it. It is as if the rushing brook flows in my veins.

Day 20

Today I slept until 9:15. The snow hangs on. A half hour of meditation flew by.

It is amazing what happens when meditation starts to take hold. An awareness is beginning to develop – an awareness of the tenor and content of my thinking. I am beginning to catch myself when I think negatively or obsessively, and especially when I project into the future. I am learning to note these thoughts, breathe into them, and let them go with the outbreath. It's new. It's fragile. But it's happening. I am learning that meditation is not about blocking things out, but instead involves letting things in, touching them lightly, and moving back to the present moment. Meditation is about acceptance of what is.

I will miss Canadian radio when I return home. This weekend, CBC is celebrating the relationship between grandparents and grandchildren, with call-in vignettes and musical requests. Hosts are finding obscure songs for old folks who used to sing such tunes as "Red Wing" and "Mockingbird Hill" to their grandchildren. Someone even asked for "Beetlebaum," a childhood favorite of mine by Spike Jones and his City Slickers.

In many ways, life in New Brunswick is similar to what I remember in the States when I was young. Although there are well-designed and modern shopping centers, a huge mall would be out of place. Children play outside unsupervised. Laundry is hung on the clotheslines, with families still enjoying that wonderful fresh-air smell in their sheets, towels, and clothing.

The old is valued. Old things and old ways are not discarded. I have spoken to New Brunswickers in their thirties who are well-educated, have had opportunities in Toronto and in the U.S., and have chosen to remain here because of the less material and simpler life style.

When I was last in the city, I spent some time at the Lancaster Mall, a small hometown shopping center. It is a hangout of sorts for senior citizens, who sit around on benches, chat, and drink coffee. Everywhere I go, I see many men and women about ten years older than myself. I am told that New Brunswick is actively seeking immigration from all over the world because of an impending major drop in population. Considering the horrendous crowding and traffic situation around Boston and on the Cape in the summer, this would seem to be a paradoxical problem. I have been to Saint John, the largest city in the province, at different times of the day, including what would be considered rush hour. I have never had a problem finding a place to park, nor have I ever been in a traffic situation where drivers have been hostile or rude. Because of this, time in town is unhasseled and pleasant.

The people of the Maritime Provinces are known for their courteousness and cordiality. I certainly can vouch for this. In the short time that I have been here, I have had two unusual business experiences. I was having trouble getting a phone card to work. The representative of the phone card company, unable to immediately correct the situation, gave me her own remaining phone card minutes. On another occasion, I forgot a bag of apples at a big market in town. When I returned the following week, I found that an employee had alerted Customer Service. There was a note at the desk instructing the clerk to replace my purchase.

~

Late winter snow hangs heavy. I notice that many trees are either uprooted or blown off at the trunk. Lots of branches sag and lean. There is nothing to be done about the tree fall. It is a natural pruning and opens space for new growth. The old goes back into the earth, giving itself to the cycle as it dies. It is nature's way of taking care of things, and there is wisdom in it.

Away from my other life, time has taken on a different quality. There is no next thing to do, so time holds no sense of pressure or urgency. There is an economy of sorts that is all-pervasive. Laws of simple living prevail. Use only the water that is needed. Consolidate the trash by tearing it into small pieces. Make do with the clothes, tools, and furnishings that are available. It is not possible to get the place toasty warm, so don't think about heat.

There is a use for everything, and nothing is unused. The stove is a one-burner hot plate from the swap shop at the dump. The coffee table is a picnic bench that was outside in Wellfleet for many years. My chair is a collapsible canvas lounge that belonged to my mother when I was a child. In my mind's eye, I can still see her as a young woman, shiny with tanning lotion, lying full face to the sun.

~

Tonight the temperature is warming considerably, and the snow is disappearing fast. Like the forest, I am making the transition to spring. My sleeping bag awaits me on the porch.

Such a way to sleep. Clean and healthy air wafts up off the Bay of Fundy. The brook babbles like a baby's lullaby. I drift off to the communication of a couple of cliff-dwelling neighbors, probably porcupines. Chatty little varmints. Like the Anasazi people of ages past, safe in a vertical refuge.

Day 21

The animals in the ledge conversed all night. I finally moved inside in the wee small hours at the onset of a thunderstorm. I didn't think that I would get wet, but I guess that I am timid about being outside during thunder and lightning. I am not sure why, as I used to take my children out onto the porch of their childhood home in the midst of storms that were so wild they would leave the smell of ozone in their wake.

I was up at 8:30. After doing my exercises, I took an anti-inflammatory for my back and attempted a little rut patching in the yard. If I move very slowly, paying attention to body mechanics, and if I quit as soon as I feel the least discomfort, I can usually accomplish things in spite of the fact that it might take a long time. This injury has worsened over the years because of my tenacious determination to undertake projects that would have been better suited to a strong man, the improper use of my back, and my unwillingness to stop when a normal day's work was completed.

This morning, songs on the radio from my parents' era catch me up short. I am swept over by a wave of nostalgia. As my mother advances into her nineties, the music of her youth has moved far into the archives, yet I remember these songs as if I first heard them yesterday. How fast my parents' lives have gone by. How close behind them I tag along.

In my journal, I grab at moments and try to anchor them down, attempting to keep them so that somehow I can have them back at a later time. I am afraid that if I don't save the past, it will be lost. It seems that there is an unacknowledged grief that is part of the condition of living – the subtle prick of truth.

I find it difficult to articulate the feeling engendered by a few words from an old song, but I believe that there is not a person who walks this earth who has not experienced it – the sadness inherent in the reality that everything changes and falls away. The only thing that we can leave behind is the tracing created by our love.

~

On this dark morning, I set out for a long walk. Strange on a day of so little color, the sea has an almost iridescent quality. Unlike the Cape, where sand and ocean dominate, the Bay of Fundy and the New Brunswick forest stand on equal footing. Pointed firs frame every seascape.

I proceed to the water and pause for a long time, leaning on my walking stick and listening to the sounds of waves running up on rock and sliding out again. The gentle washing of ancient tides put me in mind of how time washes the slate clean.

Pausing at the end of a logging road, I look out over a hilly little peninsula and beyond to lightly breaking surf and the sea. I don't know if I have ever felt so totally alone. I have the impulse to check behind me in order to make sure that I am safe, but I quickly breathe into the momentary fear and surrender to the starkness of it all.

People often ask me if I am lonely or afraid all by myself in the woods. In the grey days of April, it is bleak and desolate here. I can't explain why I love it so, but somehow the solitude and dreariness provide an indescribable sense of comfort and solace.

As I stand, facing the sea – the mist in my face and enveloped in the heavy, hanging Fundy air – all perspective changes. In my smallness and fragility, I am like a filament against the timeless landscape. I crave aloneness such as this as a suffocating person gasps for air. No, I am not afraid, except for the occasional momentary start from animal movement in the brush. No, I am not lonely. The dark time of April here at the Little Dipper is meant to be spent alone.

After a little knitting and some reading, I go to bed – inside tonight.

Day 22

I awake at 4:30 A.M. to an unusual brightness in the room. I open the door to a breathtaking scene.

The moon is full and paper white – hung in a black sky. The tiny patch of sea visible from my doorway is silver. The pointed firs stand in silhouette. The only sound is the chorus of spring peepers. Interludes like this give me to understand why there is poetry and art. Ordinary words cannot convey these experiences in a way that does justice to their beauty and impact. Poets and artists create from the mental space that aches to tell. The Buddhists would say, "Breathe with it. You are part of it." That's all.

I arise at 8 A.M. to the first beats of the sea. This morning there is one lonely peeper, freezing his little butt off – only able to get off a few feeble peeps here and there.

Hey, little fella! You have no idea how welcome you are.

The pond is now awash with algae – a primordial soup of sorts. Neon green, slimy stuff lying on the bottom. Black, jelly-like blobs floating on the surface and dragging clear protoplasmic trails, with a dark green, stringy substance mixed in. Every sunny day quadruples the quantity of it all. I hope that the little peeping frog doesn't get lost in there. Whatever will all this become?

My sleeping bag fits perfectly either in the middle of the floor or on the porch. There is enough clothing for a two months' stay. For trash disposal, I use empty plastic one-gallon water bottles into which I stuff most everything that I discard. There is a tiny bathroom, which boasts of a chamber pot and a porta-potty for guests (if anyone besides Betty Ann and my daughter-in-law Mary would ever want to stay here in these circumstances). Soon there will be an outhouse – a step up for sure.

I have a fire extinguisher, a first aid kit, towels and face cloths, a washbasin, soap, shampoo, and even some candles. What else could anyone possibly need? When I return to Wellfleet after staying here, I feel as if I have entirely too much space and too many things. I think of my daughters, Kim and Ann, and how they also efficiently make do in their warm and cozy small homes.

Today, as I walk, I am thinking about my work and a commonality in many of the lives that I have passed through. It seems that, when things are really bad, the inclination is to run away – into diversion – into a substance – into addictive behavior of some sort – into solitude. But eventually, for some of us, there is no longer any place to run, and we must stand face-on with "No!" "No. These people whom you love can not understand." "No. It can not be fixed." "No. There is no Santa Claus."

Has coming here been a form of running away? Did Thoreau go to Walden as a seeker? Or was he running away? Both?

By the time that I am ready for bed, the temperature has risen significantly. Tonight is another warm foretaste of spring, as chatterers and croakers are added to the peeping chorus. They are going at it enthusiastically when they are joined by porcupines, with their squeaky-door sound systems. As I spread my sleeping bag on the porch, I wonder if I will be able to sleep at all with such a robust chorus – a vocal gathering of spring's new creation.

Day 23

I arise today to a few weak croaks and peeps and a constellation of stars reflected in the pond. This morning I fall into a reverie. This happens alot here, perhaps because my mind is not so occupied with the circumstances of my other life. Tomorrow is the beginning of the last full week of this trip. Today, I am remembering endings.

I have often tried to articulate a feeling that I experience when special times with those I love come to an end. I remember a long-ago Labor Day weekend in Wellfleet. My son Craig and his wife Mary were there with baby Nicole. John was there with his best friend Mark, and daughter Linda was accompanied by a boyfriend. Daughter Kathy brought along a friend, whose name I do not recall. We were all packed into the tiny house. It was family togetherness at its best. Barefoot, we walked down the street and through the oncoming tide to the bridge. We sat on the Great Beach under the full moon. Mary created a phosphorescent light in the sand with a motion of her hands. And then – they all left at the same time on Tuesday morning. I sat there, physically stunned.

My grandson Dane and I traveled cross-country together. After four weeks on the road, we arrived at the home of Betty Ann in Taos, New Mexico. We visited with her for two days, and then the three of us drove to Albuquerque to put Dane on a plane in order for him to return home to Massachusetts for his birthday. As I watched him walk down the long hallway to board his flight, I felt as if all of my blood had drained to my feet. I was no good for two days.

I remember an all-adult Thanksgiving celebrated with Mom, daughter Kim and her friend from the South, son John and his wife Amy, daughter Linda, my friend Marion, and her daughter Liza. We ended the fun-filled day standing in a circle, enthusiastically singing patriotic songs. And suddenly the day was over and they all left. The silence descended like a funeral drape.

Several years ago, Linda and her children Alyssa and Mark camped at the Audubon Sanctuary with me for the first time. Kathy's son Derrick stayed for the week with us. With no electronic devices, these children invented games. Running and cavorting, they had good old-fashioned fun. We ate family meals in a screen house and slept in tents. I am a Volunteer Naturalist for the Sanctuary, and I walk the trails in the off-season. I avoided the campground for a time after our idyllic week. I finally gathered up the courage to return to Site One. I stood there amongst the tiny ghosts – lost.

And then there was a Fourth of July eve on the beach in Wellfleet with two-year old Sydney sitting on my lap – close against the cool night – as we watched the yearly fireworks display. We cheered together as we called out colors. Blue! Hurray!! Green! Red! Yea!!! Then the finale. And then it was over, colors dissolving into yet another ending. Next year, she will be three. First fireworks are a one-shot deal.

John speaks of looking back at Amy's father Joe, standing in the driveway when John and Amy drove off, bag and baggage, to start their lives together in Washington, D.C. Joe has felt the same gasp of bittersweet recognition. This will never come again – not the same way – ever.

On this early spring day, I walk a long wooded path. Green is breaking through on the fringes. Walking can be a rich source of meditation here. All walking surfaces are earthen; back to ground where, eventually, we will all return. I breathe in the substance of it. Breathing out, I let go into it.

~

The snowshoe hare was waiting for me when I came back to the Dipper. A short time ago she greeted me in her white coat, and now she is showing herself in brown and white tweed. Before I leave, she will probably be mostly summer-brown. What an amazing phenomenon – this seasonal color change. How does it happen? Just another miracle to me.

As evening fell, I listened to the music of the Maritimes. Step dancing, to the accompaniment of a fiddle and piano, is popular in Nova Scotia, and, at most public events around here, the fiddle is prominent. Because of the large French population, particularly further north in Moncton and on the Acadian Peninsula, accordion music is frequently heard. I especially enjoy listening to Rita MacNeil, a down-home diva from Cape Breton, who writes and performs her own music. Nicole and I visited Rita's Tea Room when we toured eastern Canada. Rita's rendition of "Home I'll Be" puts into words some of the feelings that I have about the Maritimes.

Day 24

Last night, the chorus was back. The croakers, the first to begin, are weakening in volume. The peepers are increasing in number and strengthening, and a new and interesting voice was added: a triller. There is a nearby pool from which the croaking sounds seem to be emanating – a pit of black, mineral-laden, standing water. This apparently draws a different kind of frog than the shallow, stream-fed, algae-filled pond.

Awakening to another grey day, I lay in my sleeping bag, pondering the music of the evening. I took an early morning ride into the village of Dipper Harbour. In this fishing community there is a breakwater, a pier, and a fish processing plant, as well as many moorings and floats. Today the tide was low and most of the boats were nicely tucked in.

Sitting for a long time, I pondered the lives of these hardy people. A father and son came ashore in a dinghy – another generation learning the trade. I have heard that fishing and logging are the most dangerous occupations.

Back at the camp, I brewed a pot of green tea, and, facing toward the meadow in my lounge chair, held the teacup to my face, breathing in the warmth of the aromatic wisps of steam. The very act of pouring the tea from the pot feels like a rite of some sort – a universal ritual going back through the ages and practiced in the most simple and elegant of circumstances, linking man to his earthen source, his forebears, and his brothers and sisters. Like so much of life that we take for granted, it is common, yet it is one of those experiences that, in our later years, we come to treasure.

How mindlessly I live so much of my life. Sometimes back in Wellfleet, when I am out on a morning walk, I am caught up short by beauty. Perhaps it is the light pooling just so, or the contrast of a dark autumn sky and low brilliant sunshine on the marsh. Most of the time, however, my mind is elsewhere. The present, the irreplaceable moment, I just thoughtlessly move on by.

So much of the time my racing mind is like a circular tape of plans, worries, and memories. Even music spins around in there. It is the motor that drives my life fast – too fast. How I would like to change this, but life-long patterns die hard. I guess that living in the day will be one of the greatest challenges of the remainder of my life.

I believe that a consistent meditation practice will help.

~

As the day ends, I head for Fundy. I love the beach when the tide is receding. I walk the wrack line, surveying the stones for a keeper. The water brings out the color and designs. Orange with blue-and-gold flecks. Black with white lines and patches. Yellow – all full of tiny holes. White polka dots on grey. Opal with lines that appear as etching on parchment. And my favorites – flat-bottomed pyramids. I have collected a fleet of them for the children. I am placing particularly interesting stones around the edge of the porch. Hopefully, guests will participate and bring back their own favorites.

The sky is cloudless. The sea is especially blue on the horizon. I love the sea. I feel as if somewhere in another life, its vast and mysterious waters have lifted me up.

The beach has changed since last summer. A large portion has been swept clean of rocks, and would be suitable for swimming. The tide begins to fall away rapidly. The stones at my feet appear to be alive as the sea rushes around them – a field of living color. Nature does not stop for a moment to allow me to catch my breath.

Out on the water, a cormorant rises up on a submerged rock and opens his wings. I spread my arms in acknowledgment, imagining a greeting. A seal rises to the surface, rolls on its side, and disappears. I go home.

I slip into my sleeping bag early. Some puffy clouds float by, top-lit pink with grey underbellies, like bubble fish drifting along. They trail off to a few wisps and dissolve.

It occurs to me that my heart has been broken.

Day 25

On this late-April day, fog hangs all about. Even the air in the cabin is moist. On my walk, I watch fog pulse through the pointed firs and onto the path. At a turn ahead, the creeping mass bursts upward and evaporates into thin air.

At the beach, it is the turn of low tide, and the air hangs with mist. The rocks are draped with seaweed, and the smell is especially musky and pungent. The only motion is a lapping movement of the water. I walk the edge, picking up stones and listening to the foghorn. I hear a far-off motor and the faint and muffled sound of a voice. I sit and breathe in the energy of this place – all soaked in sea. I love a foggy day. There is a closed-in feeling that is hard to describe. It engenders a sense of intimacy, even when I am alone.

As the afternoon progresses, the weather slowly clears. I take a walk to peek at new construction of a year-round house. It is being built on an oceanfront lot, so it will not be visible from the road. I have mixed feelings about new homes in the area. I hate to see anything change, but these folks seem to be very nice. And there is a certain inevitability about it. I am working on becoming more accepting of things as they are. This will be good practice.

At the end of the day, I spend some time planning for my mother's upcoming ninetieth birthday party. I then do a little knitting, and eventually zip myself into my sleeping bag. With days like this is it any wonder that I am as relaxed as a Raggedy Ann?

Day 26

I listened to the radio as I exercised. The situation in the Middle East is violent and bloody, and it isn't going to go away soon. My beautiful young grandsons are much on my mind.

I don't presume to know what should be done. There are no easy solutions, but I believe that military force (as in "us versus them") is not, in and of itself, the answer. When we get stuck in our own rut, we can no longer see the road.

Yes, I am concerned for those dear to me, especially the children, but also for other children far away. When my grandson Kurt was a small boy, we stayed overnight in a log cabin by a lake. Kurt met a little Russian child named Yuri, and, although they could not converse, they managed to understand each other in the marvelous universal language of children. As I watched them, my heart all but burst with gratitude. If things had turned out differently, they might have grown from being sweet little boys playing together in the sand with their trucks into enemies on the battlefield.

Sitting with a cup of tea and rereading parts of this journal, I observed all the references to "I" and "my," and reflected on our propensity to define the operation of the universe on the basis of "my needs" and "our best interests." Who are "we" really? My family and me? The neighborhood? My friends and social circle? The town? State? The country? Maybe all the people who live in congruence with our beliefs and culture? The world is bleeding. Am I not wounded also? Now there is some food for thought.

~

As this was to be my last Sunday in New Brunswick until I return in August, I took a trip into town to say good-bye to the Unitarians. Caroline and Tony volunteered to show me around the city of Saint John. Beryl told me of a meditation group at her home, and her husband John invited me to attend an evening of drumming at Gothic Arches. George promised that I would receive a monthly copy of *The Fundy Wave*, the UU newsletter, when I return to the Cape. I was introduced to Lars and Betty, who live not far from me in Seeleys Cove. They invited me to come for tea.

On the way home, I stopped at Irving Nature Park. Friends told me about this gift to the people of New Brunswick from J.D. Irving, Limited., a large, multi-faceted Canadian corporation based in Saint John. I passed over a barrier beach and parked at the bottom of a hill on this beautiful spring day.

From what I observed, there were two major circular trails on the peninsula section of the park, one wide and suitable for one-way vehicular traffic, and the other a hiking trail, wending its way along the rock cliffs. Other paths seemed to pass into the interior forest.

Prepared for a vigorous walk, I began at a good clip, swinging my arms and moving out briskly. At the top of a hill, I came upon an information kiosk and an outdoor amphitheater. Continuing on, I encountered families and joggers on the main route and hikers emerging from the less-traveled seaside trail. The views out over the rocks to the water were magnificent.

On I went, removing my jacket and anticipating arrival back at my starting point. I began to tire, as I usually do after about three miles. This pristine piece of New Brunswick is not the small city park that I had envisioned. I arrived back at the car after what felt like double my daily walking distance, impressed with this gorgeous sanctuary so close to the city of Saint John.

Returning home, I passed a stand of pussy willow. I picked a small sprig and reflected on new life, here at the Dipper and back in Dedham, where folks await the advent of New Baby. The cycle turns.

I settled into my sleeping bag on this dark night. Appearing as if swathed in cheesecloth, the waning moon was cast in a halo of mist in a sky of lavender-grey as it rose over the ledge. There was no sound. Nothing moved. All silent. All silent.

Day 27

Last night, there was another dusting of snow. Winter just does not want to quit.

I am suspended in time here. Day flows into day. The rhythm of the natural world is unbroken. Nature is a seamless garment. Sun arises from darkness in a smooth movement. Stars appear. They come and go. It is all one macrocosm rolling on – season to season.

My style of life would probably seem strange to most people, especially in this twenty-first century. Back in Wellfleet, I sleep in an unheated room, allowing my body to adapt to the change of seasons. During the winter months it is cold. I put on extra covers, and I am perfectly comfortable. I am seldom ill, as my respiratory tract is not constantly bombarded with air that is hot and dry. Other than on the coldest nights of the year, I keep a window open. How wonderful to draw in deeply the clean and moisture-laden outside air as my first conscious act of the day.

I do not have an air conditioner. In the summer I occasionally sweat. I have heard that sweating is a healthy, toxin-eliminating response to heat. We are creating temperature-controlled bubbles in which to live and work at the expense of our environment. In my childhood there was no air-conditioning. Dad wore a straw hat and an open-collared shirt. Mom made lots of lemonade. We had a fan.

Modern man has had a run of it. What with the emerging new technologies, it would seem that there is nothing that we humans can't do or fix – no problem that we cannot solve, no force that we cannot control. But nature is bigger than us. Our behavior seems to be changing some patterns in the natural world, but ultimately nature will absorb insult, adjust, and move on. The extinction of the human species would not interrupt a single sunrise.

Eating breakfast slowly and meditatively, I look out into the meadow. There is a beautiful stand of birch trees about fifty feet this side of the property line. I am appreciative that, during the logging operation, Darren saw fit to bypass them. I ponder the fact that I own these trees and all of the woods around them. In all of nature, I have the closest relationship with trees. Since way back I have found great peace sitting with particular trees through the seasons. To think of trees as mine to dispose of as I see fit seems strange – almost wrong somehow. I prefer to think of myself as steward of the earth where they are rooted.

There is an oak tree outside of my bedroom window in Wellfleet. We have a silent exchange going on. I exhale what she needs. She inhales. She exhales and releases the stuff of my sustenance. We are locked in a sacred balance. Sometimes, when I project into the future, I reflect on the possibility of a room in a nursing home with a window that can be opened to the fresh air and that looks out upon a tree as not a bad place for my last days.

~

I went to the pay phone for an hour of calls. Catching up. Winding down. Odds jobs at the cabin plus a good clean-up took till noon.

Sitting on the porch, I read from the *dharma*. This wisdom is helpful in very practical ways. The great teachers suggest that the difficulties of this world are the ground upon which our journeys take place. Practice is to sit *zazen* in spite of negative feelings and to be open to what they have to teach. I am such a beginner at this. Maybe by the time my life is over, I will have reached first base.

The sun peeks in and out. I take a long walk on logging roads and paths, and then I go to Patty's house. As always, she is hospitable and warm, ensconced in her apron by her big black iron stove.

We walk through her exquisite gardens, visit with her farm animals, and hear the first white-throated sparrow of the season sing, "Oh, sweet Can-a-da, Can-a-da, Can-a-da."

I then return to the cabin and sit in my lounge chair to watch a front move in. I position myself to look into the grove. Fast-moving clouds rush by on the horizon. Merging. Blending. Dispersing. Trailing ribbons in their wake. All shapes and shades of grey passing below big white puffies, and opening to reveal patches of blue.

Now the entire sky turns battleship blue-grey. The birches look painted on, highlighted in bold white by the setting sun. Black storm clouds materialize and race across the sky as the sun disappears. A strong wind comes up. The birches begin to dance. And now it is raining, pelting the cabin, driven by this out-of-nowhere wind, now whistling in the trees. And now the thunder and lightning begin. I unplug my two electric heaters and sit back down to watch.

The wind breaks the surface of the pond into tiny ripples, moving in kaleidoscopic waves, sometimes affecting the entire surface and other times darting here and there in the shape of spears. When the wind dies down a bit, the surface roils like water about to boil. And now, out of the side window, a break — bright sky on the horizon. It is just about time for sunset. All this for free!

A can of chickpeas along with a can of artichoke hearts and a handful of roasted sunflower seeds, eaten mindfully against such a backdrop, is bliss.

As the sun went down, I was visited once again by the bunny, this time for a really long while. She sat under my window, munching on newly emerging green grass – content and peaceful. I could see the detail in her beautiful velvety ears. The size of a cat, with huge back feet and a loping gait, she has a tiny white cottontail and big brown eyes. She has almost attained her summer coloration, except for white areas on her paws and belly. She stayed and stayed, browsing the yard. When I went to sleep, she was still there.

Day 28

This morning, the squawking of crows awakens me. I find them to be the most interesting of birds. Sociable and intelligent, they seem to engage in rituals. One time I witnessed a group of crows assembled in a circle, making loud clicking sounds, nodding and turning in place. In a behavior known as "mobbing," they dive en masse at large birds, particularly owls and hawks. Apparently they use harassment as a policing method. This morning, it sounds as if something urgent is going on.

Meditation deepens. Three times a day now, and I am looking forward to it. Concepts in the *dharma* books that have heretofore been total mysteries are now beginning to make sense. It seems that complexity is being reduced to simplicity. I lie down to meditate under a cloud-covered sky and arise to warm, bright sunshine. Today I simply watch breathing happening . . . breathing happening . . . breathing happening . . . .

As I write this, I observe two small towels on the clothesline in the brilliant sunshine, flapping in the breeze. I cannot see the wind but it has great power, especially when engaged with a supple contact.

~

I went to lunch today at Fundy Haven, a small restaurant in the village of Dipper Harbour. The food was great, especially Ruby's homemade soup.

This afternoon, I sat by the window in the little alcove watching the snow turn to rain and then back to snow again – contented, quiet, at rest. When I arrived here, I had a question on my mind regarding what I might do in a particularly difficult and important situation. I am learning that questions don't necessarily have immediate answers, and that sometimes it is necessary to carry the question for a long while. Sometimes it is necessary to wait. After this extended time here, the answer is still not clear, but it has become easier to live with the question.

I remember a story told by a woman at a self-help meeting. It seems that she had some beads that were all jumbled up. She struggled to untangle them. Finally, exasperated, she put them in her pocket. Later, as she reached in for a handkerchief, the beads fell on the floor, becoming disentangled as they landed. Sometimes we are powerless – and waiting is the only thing to do. And letting go. Letting go.

As the day progressed, it warmed substantially. Once again, I went to the beach. The tide was high. As the sun set, the lights from the Point Lepreau Generating Station cast a glow in the sky on the horizon. This nuclear facility provides many jobs for local residents. Hidden away, its existence would not be apparent to someone passing through.

When I first came here, I was uncomfortable with its presence. There is that old "What if . . . ?" mentality, in which I have lived so much of my life. The underlying emotion is fear. I have been here awhile, and I am no longer afraid. I guess it is like so many other issues in life: the cure for fear is familiarity.

Nuclear power is certainly a cleaner source of energy than fossil fuels, but what is the trade off? In the U.S., I also live in proximity to a nuclear power plant. Located in the Town of Plymouth (where the Pilgrims are purported to have landed), it is less than thirty miles away, as the crow flies. In Canada and the U.S. many millions of people, including all but three of my children and grandchildren, live within forty-five miles of nuclear plants. I cannot say that I am afraid for us. Rather, I have a pervasive sense of uneasiness.

On the Cape, there is much current controversy regarding the erection of wind turbines in Nantucket Sound. Property and pleasure boat owners object to the presence of these large structures in their 'front yard,' so to speak. But what are we to do? I would prefer to look at a wind turbine than risk the environmental and physical dangers of other options.

Of course, we could always conserve . . . .

~

Towards 9 P.M., as I sat in the cabin reading, the most amazing thing happened. The croaking frogs, the peepers, and the trillers were joined by a kind of clicking sound. I went out onto the porch to listen. And then a raspy scraping was added. A stereophonic soundscape of frogdom. I stood there – laughing out loud!

April has been a wonderful month to be here. All nature is awakening from its winter sleep. Habitats such as this are being destroyed in the unrelenting march of development. In putting in the pond, I have created a habitat. All that needed to be done was to dig a hole along the course of a stream, construct a dam, and wait.

I am serenaded to sleep tonight by the music of nature. Twenty, thirty, or more strong voices of tiny creatures, all singing out the joy of being, all complete in their spring frog essence. It is a celebration – a celebration of life. No symphony has ever been more beautiful.

Each existence is here only for a day, as am I. We are all impermanent – just passing through – but the song goes on. Dare I to believe that a higher power has arranged this place? This very night? Or is all of this simply a combination of randomness and my own creative action?

In any event, here I am, enraptured by the volume of sheer exuberance that engulfs me. Here we all are – connected. The frogs and the listener. The spring earth and the pointed firs. The universal breath. Yes, and even my other life. Maybe especially my other life.

Day 29

I am roused by the sound of work from the harbor, the radio of a passing fishing boat, and the smell of hamburgers. Whatever is it like out there – bobbing about in a world of unobstructed sky? How is it to be able to see storms materialize on the horizon and to know that they lie between yourself and home?

I stretch out my body and hold this position, creating space in my spine. It feels really good. My breath rises and falls. Long breaths. Deep breaths. I am astonished at how late I can stay down in the morning. Even after waking, I just loll around, luxuriating in this state of peace. There is no possibility of intrusion by the telephone and no doing to be done. Just rest. Total rest. Lying on my back in deep meditation, it feels as if my body, my jaw, and all the muscles and skin of my face are sinking into the floor.

Today, I followed an old path, which I was told might lead to a beaver pond. Hiking in New Brunswick is different from walking the trails at the Audubon Sanctuary, where I volunteer back on the Cape. In spite of the fact that it is Audubon policy to allow nature to take its course, the Sanctuary trails are well-maintained. The paths through the woods here are overgrown. I whack my way through.

Tonight, I retired late, and the scene that greeted me when I went out onto the porch literally took my breath away. The moon was lying low behind white clouds. Three large pointed firs stood in silhouette. There was no sound. The moon went in and out, as gauzy clouds passed by. Then a raspy *S-crick, S-crick, S-crick* of some small creature broke the silence. This cloud cover passing this moon behind these pointed firs has never happened before and will never happen again in exactly the same way. The insect has already moved on. I need to watch. I must watch.

Day 30

This morning, fair weather cumulus clouds are breaking up, forming wispy designs. Grey is moving in.

I met Caroline and Tony in town for a guided tour. They actually used to be tour guides for passengers on the cruise ships that dock in Saint John. I much enjoy these congenial folk and especially appreciate Tony's thick British accent. Both Caroline and Tony were born in England, immigrated to the States, and ended up here in New Brunswick. Tony is a citizen of all three countries.

We began with lunch at Holly's, a lovely promenade-side café in Market Square. Situated on the harbor, with both outdoor and indoor entertainment areas, Market Square is the site of many local performances and festivals. The two-level indoor mall hosts many stores, as well as a large public library and the New Brunswick Museum.

We then took a walk along the new waterfront pedway, and proceeded up through a large hotel and back through Market Square to the Aquatic Center. A walking promenade extends up the hill connecting the Aquatic Center, City Hall, and Brunswick Square, a multi-level indoor shopping mall. A corridor connects to City Market, which fronts King's Square, a park-like open area complete with a fountain, benches, and pigeons.

We then went to a section referred to as Trinity Royal. There are several streets of brick homes, old and well-maintained. The neighborhood is immaculate and the doorways are particularly elegant.

Roofs on most all of the buildings are flat. During the conflagration back in the 1870's, many people who were trapped in wooden houses lost their lives. When Saint John was reconstructed, consideration was given to fire safety in the design of new structures.

Trinity Church was our next stop. We viewed the Coat of Arms that the Loyalists brought here from Boston when they fled the Revolution. The ownership remains controversial, in a good-natured and humorous way.

Teenagers and young adults were in evidence everywhere, sitting in the park eating lunch, congregating in Market Square, skateboarding in an enclosed cement area, or just ambling around. Groups of smaller children seemed to be on field trips, visiting the various historical sites or headed to the Aquatic Center for recreation. The major high schools for the area extending all the way down to Dipper Harbour and beyond are in Saint John, and the University of New Brunswick is nearby.

We continued by car, with Caroline and Tony's beloved Golden Labrador, Sandford, and drove to Mispec, just beyond industrial Saint John. The coastline is beautiful. At Cape Spencer, it is possible to see Nova Scotia across the Bay of Fundy.

New Brunswick is bilingual, with both English and French appearing on such things as road signs, labels, and printed material. Caroline and Tony told me of the Samuel de Champlain Community Centre, named after the explorer who discovered the area on Saint John the Baptist Day. On the way home, I paid the place a visit. There is a day care and a kindergarten through grade twelve school, a theater, and a library. Everything is presented in French, including the posters on the walls.

I reflected on the names of the towns and streets. Miramichi. Pocologan. Quispamsis. Manawagonish. They have a Native ring to them. The Natives of Canada are referred to as the First Nation People. The Maliseets and Micmacs are indigenous to New Brunswick, and there is a relatively large Native settlement in Fredericton. Their opinions are respected and especially sought-after on matters of the environment.

~

Back at the Dipper, as I settle down for the evening, it is clear that the struggle with myself is beginning again. I am mentally gearing up to leave and contemplating the many tasks to be done when I arrive home. The switch has been flipped, and my racing mind is on full speed ahead. Meditation is becoming a challenge, to say the least. I will have to remember the advice of the sages. Now is when the real work of practice is done. Count breaths if I need to. Do anything that helps, but don't quit.

In the States, another little person will soon be here. Bing Crosby, a performer from the 1930's and 40's and the father of a large family, commented on the miracle of love, and how, with every new person who is added, love is multiplied – like the Scriptural loaves and fishes. It is inexhaustible. My heart could burst from the fullness of it all.

Day 31

Today is as cold as it was when I arrived. My feet are freezing. I have taken off and packed my wool socks and heavy sweater. I am wearing all the clean winter clothes that I have left in order to stay warm. The weather has come in from the west. I believe that they call it an Alberta Clipper, a cold front moving through like a freight train. I hope that the baby frogs don't freeze.

This morning, my carpenter, Kevin, arrived with the outhouse, a solidly constructed one-seater. Chatting for a bit, he told me a little family history. His recently deceased father had a milling business, perhaps the source of Kevin's roots in wood. It seems that his Dad particularly revered three ancient fir trees that stand on the edge of Musquash Marsh. Kevin said that they may be Norwegian Spruce. They are taller than the surrounding forest and are visible on Route 1 just before the Musquash turn-off. I will think of Kevin's father every time that I see them.

This month away – the seclusion, the quiet, the utter simplicity – has been pure gift. Experiencing my place in the interweaving of the natural world puts my life and death in perspective. I am not a big deal, yet I am vital in the continuation of the sacred circle. I live my little life and I die, like all the other interconnected elements of this mystical web. I change form and move on.

I spent most of the day preparing to leave – cleaning, packing, and planning the first week of my return to the States. I kept the radio going in the background, and was caught up short by a banjo rendition of "Waiting for the Sunrise." Dad played that song so skillfully. Sometimes he and Dick, his long-time friend, would perform publicly, and they would bring down the house, especially when they played their banjos behind their heads.

Dad and I were especially bonded through music. At a young age I became adequately proficient to play the accordion or piano along with him. Did I ever feel like a big deal when Daddy and I played the songs of the 20's and 30's together.

I especially remember Dad encouraging me to appreciate good music. I can still see the old hall and the upright piano on which I would practice when I tagged along with him on workdays. And there's the music book, and my little fingers playing the left hand melody of "Kamenoi Ostrow," which he so enjoyed - and "Intermezzo." I can hardly bear to listen to it. I can still see him standing next to me and saying, "Marlene, this is beautiful music." And it was. Daddy was my mentor, my funny playmate, and my pal, and he lives on, as will Mom, as long as I am here to remember.

It is amazing how much passes through our lives and is forgotten the same day, yet simple incidents from sixty years ago can seem so fresh in memory. I can see Mom sitting on a chair in my bedroom, reading from the book, *Heidi*. I remember how I looked forward to another chapter each night. I can still see the room, and her, and even the cover of the book. I can smell the freshness of the sheets, and I can see my mother bending over to tuck me in, as the "William Tell Overture" announced the beginning of my all-time favorite radio program, "The Lone Ranger." In spite of the fact that she was every inch a lady, she never discouraged my tomboy inclinations. Thanks, Mom.

Tonight I tackled the packets of readings – including magazines, newspaper clippings, and periodicals – given to me by my Canadian friends. Like Betty Ann, Tom, my Wellfleet neighbors Shirley and Paul, and my other close friends from the States, these folks are well-read, particularly on international issues and the environment.

Amazingly, Mom has done O.K. without me while I have been away. At almost ninety years of age, she gets herself to the market and around town on errands. She functions independently, managing her own finances and making all of her own decisions. She has diabetes, high blood pressure, and high cholesterol, but everything seems to be under the control of medication. If she is having any major aches and pains, she sure is fooling me. I am proud of her.

~

This last full night here, I sit on the porch and play my flute to the pond. The baby frogs start to sing – really!

In the early evening, I drive to the Dipper Harbour docks, watch the boats come in and unload the day's catch. The sunset materializes all around me, while little Canadian boys play on the rocks. I am writing this in my car by the pier as the day and my April retreat come to an end.

Time to go – and just as I was beginning to develop a pattern of pothole avoidance in order to effectively negotiate the spring ruts on the way in to the Little Dipper.

SUMMER

Day 1

As always, the ride up was long, but great!

The AirLine (Route 9) through rural Maine is scenic and interesting. The road itself is winding and hilly, with occasional breakthrough views of the countryside. There are tiny villages and a bear-hunting lodge. The Canadian border guards have warned me that there have been many moose collisions and that this is a dangerous route, especially at night.

After I crossed the border and got underway on Route l, the last leg of the nine-hour trip, I began to slip into a process that is becoming familiar – questioning myself as to why I have chosen to come so far from Wellfleet. As soon as I pulled into the path leading up to the Dipper, however, I remembered why I am here.

For the rest of the day, I was busy with the small chores associated with opening the cabin. Then, as seems to happen every visit when the frenetic activity of packing, traveling, and unpacking are completed, I have this mini-crash and become nostalgic. Tonight I am remembering myself as a child.

I always did well in school, and when I would bring home a glowing report card, Dad would ask, "Are you first in your class?" I would answer, "First – or second." "Why not first?" would be my father's reply. I tried harder.

In the summer here it is cooler than in the States, but warm enough to sleep on the porch. The moon is full this week, and tonight it is turning the pond to silver. The moonlight is so bright that the trees are actually casting shadows. I rise to step out into the yard in the middle of the night. It is a fairyland. I am acutely conscious of being the only human in the presence of all this life. Shining in the moonlight. Shining. We are all shining.

Day 2

As dawn breaks, I rise and go into the house, brew coffee, and sit with my hands around the cup . . . remembering . . . remembering . . .

Back home, the beautiful new baby is here, and her name is Julia. Plans are moving ahead for Mom's ninetieth birthday party in September. It will be a surprise. Craig, Mary, Nicole, and Aaron are coming from Seattle. How very special.

I spend most of the day doing odds and ends and preparing a big batch of soup. As I sit down tonight to read, I choose *Nothing Special* by Charlotte Joko Beck. This is a second re-read for me, as I have found this Zen book to be very informative regarding principles by which I am striving to live.

I also reread a perennial favorite: *The Other Way to Listen* by Byrd Baylor and Peter Parnall. A children's book suitable for any age, it is a simple and easy-read primer of mindfulness.

I go to bed early. It is so nice to be back out on the porch – open to the movement of the natural world.

Day 3

Last night was eerie. As I scrunched into my sleeping bag, thunderstorms were rolling all around. There were strange, shrill animal sounds from the ledge. Breezes shifted this way and that. Lightning flashes burst like bombs over the Bay of Fundy. I could feel the electricity in the air. An all-pervasive energy surrounded me, and I was penetrated by it.

I awoke early. Dawn broke through the overcast, at first in a small bright blue patch and then in larger openings.

As I took a brief morning walk, I came upon a rock with a superimposed battered heart – wet from the early morning dew. I put it in my pocket to add to the growing collection on the porch. As I walked

"I went to Fundy. I was spellbound by the show."

"I walk the quiet paths ...

...as I let New Brunswick have its way with me."

"Fall color ... is a combination of muted shades of yellow and rust and the four season green of fir."

"I came upon an abandoned tiny house, poised at the edge of a cove."

"The door was open, so I went in."

"It seems that life of all kinds thrives on the edges ...

*...the places of contrast where dark meets light
- the places of change."*

"Consider the seventh generation to come ...

(Pictured - The island of Grand Manan)

... rising up through the ground."

(Pictured - Chance Harbour)

"There must be something unique in the character of a fisherman - formed by a life at sea and fed by the necessity of adaptation, ingenuity, and courage."

(Pictured - Dipper Harbour)

"The ceiling is constructed in the form of an inverted ship's hull, so much in keeping with the sea-orientation of this Maritime Province."

(Pictured - City Market, Saint John)

*"For folks here the sea runs thick in the blood ...
compelling, familiar,
and dark as the rocks upon which they live."*

"New shoots from old roots"

"Then came my favourite event - the lobster crate races."

(Pictured - Fundy Fishermen Days, Dipper Harbour)

*"New shoots
from old roots"*

(Pictured - Fundy
Fisherman Days,
Dipper Harbour)

"The doorways are particularly elegant"

(Pictured - The city of Saint John)

"The merchants seem to take pride in maintaining the ambience of a welcoming and inviting main street."

(Pictured - The village of St. Andrews)

"The Boyce Farmers' Market exceeded all my expectations."

"... red-coated soldiers ... march through town in order to keep the tradition established by the First Royal Regiment."

(Pictured - The city of Fredericton)

"Pausing at the fork in the road, I regard a small white building ... Solid, unpretentious, enduring, it is characteristic of these people and this place that I have come to love."

"It is the community of blazing life that takes my breath away."

(Pictured - Looking down from the second floor of Market Square)

*"A blessing.
Toward me? Toward
Dipper Harbour?
Toward the sea?"*

85

*"I have become a tissue of senses.
I breathe with the forest. My heart beats with the sea."*

"Healing rises up through the roots here."

*"Ethereal ... like this day - this place
... I remember."*

"See the bunny, Emma ..."

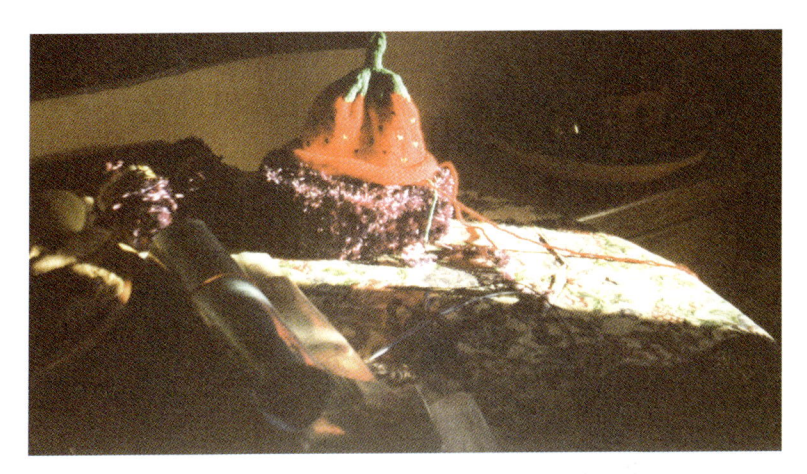

"I finished New Baby's strawberry hat."

"As I settle into sleep, I reflect on the mystery of it all - the whole of it - the dance."

"... here only for a moment, only for a day ..."

along, the experience of the evening remained with me, hanging in the air, manifesting as a compelling sense of presence.

As evening falls, a line of clouds hangs dark on the horizon – like a window shade opening on a living landscape. Under the shade, a sunset materializes. Pink is added. And now gold. A large flock of birds flies off under the drape toward Fundy. Sitting quietly, I feel the first stirring of the night air – a tiny current carrying the fresh smell of the sea.

Day 4

Last night was cool and, unlike the night before, totally still and silent. Not a leaf moved. Not a bell buoy or a foghorn sounded. Even the sea itself was bereft of sound. The woods were black. A sky of twinkling stars was reflected in the glassy metallic pond. The only stirring was the occasional croak of a frog.

There is a vastness in this silence. It is as deep as the space that I gaze out into. All infused by the same energy. All poised as if in expectant anticipation – and yet deeply peaceful. The very lightest of movements, barely discernable, lifts air to my face. Clean. Fresh. Cool. A frog hops into the water. *Splash!* I am enchanted. I have arrived.

This morning, I left early for a long walk. The wood thrush called out his magical melody from the woods along the path. Out on the main road, Native People were gathering rushes from the roadside to weave baskets.

Along the way, a woman in her driveway mistook me for someone else who walks the main road frequently. We talked for a time, and she introduced herself as Lynn.

On the way home, I came across a baby bird floundering about in the middle of the path. I gently picked it up to move it to the side, but, before I put it down, we gazed at each other for a moment. Am I crazy, or what? As its tiny heart beat against my fingers, I felt that same energy – the energy of the night.

In the late afternoon, I spend two hours lying on the porch in sweet peace. Not asleep. Not quite awake. Just here in this present moment. Two snowshoe hares in their brown summer coats nibble

on the grass. One even comes up on the deck.
Emma . . . see the bunnies . . .

Day 5

During the night the fog rolled in. This morning, rock music from a passing fishing boat seems like a very short distance away.

Today, as I am writing this, I am sitting on the porch. The breeze gently stirs the pond. Whirligig beetles create ever-widening circles on the water, breaking the reflection of the white clouds. They gather together in a large group, pause for a time, and then burst out, chasing each other across the pond in seemingly aimless patterns.

How long before the whirligigs complete their cycles? What will become of the baby bird? And me? The present moment is all we really have. We can plan for more, but, in the incessant planning, we lose the fragile gift of *now*.

I watch a big brown frog leap across the pond bank, perch on the edge, and hop in. Zen Buddhists see frogs in their alert position as the perfect meditators. Dragonflies cruise the pond, while the whirligigs continue to engage in their antics. A real show-off performs a zigzag routine, creating a magnificent wake, while a full gallery of brothers and sisters look on.

What to call it, this energy? I am waiting on a name. I question the wind, the frog, the tide: what source do you ride?

~

Today, on my trip to the payphone, I had the occasion to call my daughter Kathy. Although the pall of grief has lifted somewhat since Emma's death, there are occasional days when she revisits the dark place. There are memories. If only's. What if's. Today was such a day. I listened and said little. What is there to say to the deep and enduring pain of a bereaved parent? All I can do is to be present and bear this loss with her.

There is more pain in store for my large family and me. There are accidents, illnesses, and – hanging ominous – there is war. I am learning that life is to be lived in the moment. Life is to be lived *now*.

I want to try to describe an awareness that is becoming increasingly sharp as I grow older. There are times, particularly with my grandchildren, that are so precious, so perfect, that I become like a bee drowning in honey. The children cannot know how deeply I am drawing in the sweetness.

Also, sometimes when I come upon parents or grandparents with small children or babies, I am overwhelmed by the depth of love manifest in the relationship. I know that, when my mother is gone, I will have lost the person in the world who loves me most of all.

I ended the day on the beach, and had some fun creating contests in anticipation of visits from my family. I see a construction game as having great promise. Large circles are to be drawn in the pebbles for each contestant, right in the path of the incoming tide. Folks (young and old) are to construct edifices with any stones that they find or can dig up within their circle, and then we will see what Fundy does to these creations. Water always wins!

As the massive Fundy tide wells up, I watch the sea take the rocks. Nothing to do. Nowhere to go. Such utter luxury.

Day 6

Crashing thunderstorms were directly overhead last night. A particularly bright flash and an almost simultaneous *R-R-Rip* prompted me to abandon my porch position, go indoors, and draw all the curtains up tight. Scared? Just a little bit. It's that all-pervasive energy again, manifesting itself in a wild outburst.

I am awakened this morning by a conversation between two warbler-type voices. Over the brush toward the sea, the pointed firs are breaking through the early morning light. The sky changes slowly from grey-black to grey-blue. Everything that has come before has led to this moment, this sleeping bag and mat, this cabin on this pathway in this country at this time. And now the song of a wood thrush far, far off. I am captivated by the movement of night to dawn.

The sun rises over the ledge, instantaneously bringing warmth. As I write this, looking out on the woods, a tiny spider drifts down on a strand from the roof. How does this happen? Is the strand pre-existent somewhere in the spider's innards? A breeze comes up. The spider hangs precariously for a time, swinging to and fro. Then, dropping rapidly to the ground, the spider disappears.

Clouds are cotton balls with distinct edges of light in a blue sky, vividly reflected in the pond.

Breathing in... breathing out... Cool air at my nostrils. The faint smell of apples from my stash on the porch. The passage of the sun as it moves down my back.

Here. I am here.

It is time to get up and get going. This is going to be a hiking day. I would like to explore new trails, further into the woods and further out along the cliffs. I set off with my trusty walking stick and with boots to protect my ankles, as I plan to get off the beaten track.

Leaving the path, I follow a ledge to a large, extraordinary meadow. Soft and squishy but not mushy, it appears to be a bog, lush with all kinds of vegetation. Surrounded by pointed firs, it is secluded. I speculate that moose must frequent the place, but the low bushes are too thick for any tracks to be visible.

Scattered throughout the meadow are plants with exotic, waxy red blossoms. The base of each stem is surrounded by oblong receptacles that seem to gather water.

As I continue on, I walk a familiar dirt road. I notice a pattern of tiny intersecting crevasses. I see that these pathways, an inch wide in some places, have been formed by the passage of tiny ants from hill to hill, village to village. One village is particularly intricate, with at least fourteen openings down into the seemingly hard-packed and solid earth. Some larger red ants are in the vicinity. One intrudes, and is promptly expelled by a tiny, fierce black warrior.

Thirty feet further down the way, there is another construction project, and then another. The path is laced with them: tiny ant metropolises on a well-worn pathway that I have walked frequently since I arrived. Have these been here all along, beneath my line of vision? Have I carelessly tread upon them as I passed over, oblivious to small strivings? And what will happen in the rain? Will the ants be sealed in gravel tombs?

Aware of time passing, I wonder how long I will be able to journey north to New Brunswick. It is a nine-hour ride from the Cape. Boston traffic is heavy. The Dipper has come late in life for me. I think of the ants. A storm in the night and heavy traffic and their lives will be changed. Mine, too.

I return to the cabin, ravenous as a bear. After a lunch of peanut butter, rice cakes, and an apple, I settle in to mid-day meditation. The ants don't worry about tomorrow. Neither will I.

I am down early tonight. Sleeping outside is a highlight of my time here. I spread a mat on the porch floor. This provides a base for my sleeping bag. That is all that I need for comfort. On long trips with my grandchildren, I learned how to be portable. I can sleep anywhere.

Rain begins, coming in from the west. It patters on the porch roof, and falls with metallic clicks on the pond. Thunder rolls in the distance, and surf sounds rise from the bay. Stereophonic nature lulls me to sleep. Together we are washed clean, the cabin and I – renewed by the outpouring of waters.

Day 7

This morning, clouds are white on powder blue. High ice crystals spin out, trailing wisps. A rib cage emerges as I watch. Now a mustached hollow face with icy hair materializes.

I am off for my walk before breakfast. Heavy rains from last night have washed out part of the path. Rivulets pour over ledges.

Wildflowers are blossoming everywhere. Yellow. Red. Pink. Lavender. One would never believe that just two years ago the landscape was brown and seemingly lifeless as the result of the logging. I purchased the lot in the coldest March weather that I have ever experienced. The land was covered with slash, but I could picture what nature had in store.

Before I came to Canada, I went to Yellowstone on an extended trip to the western U.S. with Kurt. A few years prior, there had been major forest fires that laid waste to vast expanses of the park. I looked out over the landscape with grief for what seemed to have been lost.

But then I learned of edges. The burn was a mosaic of sorts. Fire flattened a large swath but left the neighboring woods untouched, much like the logging operation, which bypassed patches and borders of trees here and there. It seems that life of all kinds thrives on the edges, the places of contrast where dark meets light – the places of change.

That made sense to me, not only in practical application to the forest, but also in my particular life. I am walking an edge. The analogy is startling.

The charred parkland will return to forest, only to burn again eventually. This small piece of northern woods but a year ago was lying as if in ruin, yet today it is bursting with new life. Life to death – from which springs new life.

I am going down. That is for sure. But not as a thrashing outsider. Instead, as a strand of an interconnected web, cast out over the edge. Cast into something incomprehensively big – into something much bigger than myself.

Day 8

I awake early on this unusually clear and blue morning. As I look out at the pond, I see a frog lazing on the surface. After a time, he dives deep and disappears. The sun rises as I watch. Night flows into day. Contentment - is this what it feels like?

~

Today I did errands. My first stop was in the city, as I wanted to pick up some birthday gifts from Canada. I stopped at the Museum and found a children's book, *East to the Sea* by Heidi Jardine Stoddart, about family visits to a seaside family home. I purchased two. I also bought *New Brunswick* by Sherman Hines, a beautiful coffee table book of photography, as a gift for Mom. She will appreciate knowing more about this place to which I disappear in the summer.

After picking up a few items at Canadian Tire, I went to a seed store on Rothesay Avenue to buy some grass and clover seed. A young woman assisted me, and spent a great deal of time making sure that I had exactly what I needed. We chatted a bit. I commented on her congeniality and courtesy. "It's the Maritime way," she responded.

I then stopped for a swim and shower at the Aquatic Center and an omelet at Cora's Breakfast & Lunch, after which I continued on to

McAllister Place, a big, single-level indoor mall, to get a sun hat and to do a little more gift shopping. I returned to town and made a circle around the industrial section of Saint John. An oil refinery is located here. A large tanker was docked at this facility today.

Before heading back through the city, I swung up to Rockwood Park, a large green space in Saint John, replete with walking trails and an interpretive center. Nicole and I camped here when we traveled the Maritimes. Today I drove to the barn to visit the horses that pull wagons and give horseback rides. I think that there is swimming, golfing, and even a zoo at Rockwood.

Riding through the city, it is easy to see why it became the largest site of business and industry in the area. A city of the sea, Saint John is rimmed by water on three sides. The Saint John River and the harbor at its mouth are impressive, to say the least. One of the world's great rivers, the Saint John is wide and powerful, driven by waters all the way from Maine. The massive Fundy tides rush in to reverse the course of the river two times every day. There is a viewing point over this spot known as Reversing Falls, and a restaurant of the same name where I have dined and watched the phenomenon.

At the end of this long day, I settle into sleep, pleased with my accomplishments and happy that I will be here at the Dipper for a while.

Day 9

Off for a walk this morning, I headed for the place where I thought that I smelled a bear previously in the spring. As I rounded a corner in an area bounded by cliffs, I came upon a bird of prey poised over a fresh kill. The bird was very large, with a dark body and a white head. I stopped. It briefly looked up and took note of me, but then continued feeding. I watched for a time, and then began to inch forward for a better look. The bird flew off, landing on a high branch of a nearby tree.

The kill was a large bird itself. Shaped like a duck, it was grey with a white stomach, short yellow legs, and taloned webbed feet. Its head had been neatly removed. As I walked further on, the predator sounded. As a Volunteer Naturalist, I have learned some birdcalls, including those of hawks. I had never heard this one before. I left the bird to its breakfast, and walked on up the road. An eagle. I think that it was an eagle.

Back at the Dipper, the pond is fast becoming a focal point of all kinds of activity. The dragonflies have appeared – tiny turquoise blue and larger red and orange. A fat green frog jumped from the shore, swept the width of the pond in two or three thrusts, and surfaced near the edge to rest on the bottom, head up, waiting for dinner. I did some tasks and returned. The frog was still there.

As night fell, summer breezes turned the birch leaves over and back again. I awoke some time near 2 A.M. The night air had a smell all its own. Sharp. Clean. The cabin creaked as it settled.

Throughout the deep night, I was in and out of sleep. As the first light of dawn broke under a sliver of moon, a bird sang three tentative notes and then added a triplet ending, announcing the new day.

Bats circled in silhouette above the ledge, picking off insects over the pond. Dark shapes flitting across the line of trees. There – one crossed the moon! As a contrail swept across the sky and dissipated into mist, I was reminded that I am moving inexorably toward my death. Interwoven into the tapestry of life, there is no stopping it. Poised like the frog, sure as the eagle – it waits to take me whole.

Day 10

This morning, I take a long walk on old logging roads. Walking through fields and woods, I am taken back to the country home where I raised my family. Memories surface. I pause, sit on a rocky knoll, and the flood begins.

Babies and tiny tots – here and gone so quickly. Horses and ponies, Underdog, Ralph the cat – swept along by time. My children. My beautiful children. It all seems like a single poignant page in a long, living novel.

I remember the little boy who spent all of his savings to buy a typewriter for me so that I would no longer have to struggle with my schoolwork on the old, broken-down version. There was the little girl who was up and out every morning through the cold winter, in order to carry warm water for the horse and pony, and who used the proceeds of her paper route to purchase their feed.

And the young woman who came into my bedroom when I was studying to show me her deep and sensitive poetry and to talk about life. And then there was the sweet, smiling, and engaging little girl, handed to me by a mysterious woman, who disembarked from an almost empty Korean airplane and then disappeared into the night.

Not to mention the determined teenager who taught herself gymnastics, and blew me away with her stellar performance at the first meet that I attended. And my big boy, the last of that golden generation of Viet Nam era youth, with his long hair, Spanish-American War jacket, bare feet, and music.

I was a child myself, far too young to have all these children of my own. I stumbled along through over two decades. I had one chance to be a parent – only one. It came and went like last night's moon. I cannot redo a moment of it.

The past has crept up and ambushed me. I finish the day in an uneasy state of mind.

Day 11

Dawn breaks with pink light rimming a low fog bank. The sun climbs over the ledge, highlighting the trees – first the crowns and then the trunks. I await its warmth. I tug at the zipper of my sleeping bag. I am in a sweatshirt and fleece. Even in July, the Canadian morning air is crisp and cool.

A noise in the pond draws my attention. Two bird-like ducks are performing some kind of ritual. They preen, shaking feathers. One stands on its tail, with wings flapping wildly. Then they drift about on the water. I sit and watch.

Without a bird book, I cannot identify them. Grey-brown on the back with small comb-like white wing bars, their bottoms are all white. Slightly darker around the eyes, they do not have a classic duckbill. They come closer and then dive below the surface. Again and again, they surface and dive.

They drift in to face one another, and then float along side-by-side, all curled up into themselves like footballs. They dive again simultaneously, leaving two interlocking circles of expanding ripples on the pond. Now they come close, diving beneath me. I see a yellow leg. One of their kind was food for the eagle.

They rise from the water together, and, in one motion, take to the air, skimming across the pond, stopping for a moment, and then flying off over the pointed firs toward the sea. No athletes ever performed more beautifully.

As the sun breaks through, I arise and leave for a walk. A few June flies remain, hovering about me when I stand still. I bewilder them with the long sleeves and hood of my lightweight, protective shirt. No matter how hard they try, they cannot get to my flesh for their bloodmeal.

I walk a trail that traverses the top of the ridge, past the white cliffs, and on to a pond. A path intersects and leads to a waterfall. Darren has planted flowers and new trees of all kinds in every nook and cranny. I continue, up over rock ridges, through the woods, and on to the bog lot. Patty informs me that the exotic flowers are known as pitcher plant.

Heading back toward the Dipper, I set out moving parallel to the sea. I stopped to ponder the view across the meadow and through the ever present pointed firs. Usually these trees arrange themselves in groupings, mostly close together in groves. Occasionally, however, a lone individual stands away from the rest. In my line of vision is such a tree. A little lop-sided and weather-beaten, it is rooted close to the bay, and has been there for many seasons. It watches. It waits. I feel kinship with it.

I walk a logging road to the back of my lot, and attempt to bushwhack the property line. The brush is particularly thick and high, but I trudge my way through until I connect with the trail to the ledge. I arrive home famished and sit for a long while over a delicious bowl of soup.

Laying down on the porch, I settle into meditation. Once again, practice is deepening, as it does each time that I come here. It usually takes several days for this to begin to happen. In the hustle and bustle of life back in the States, I don't seem to be able to keep a daily time set aside to turn off my busy mind. Here, in the silence and stillness, I am able to watch the thinker and not get lost in the thought.

Day 12

On this dreary day, I am aroused by the intermittent sound of the foghorn. I get into my rain gear and take a slow, drizzly walk. The fragrances of the summer woods and the sea accompany me. On damp days, the smells are especially sweet and pungent. Maybe that is why I don't mind the rain and the fog. In some ways, I prefer bleak weather.

Everything is still, as the drizzle becomes more constant. The pointed firs stand straight and tall against the heavy, grey sky. Silent sentinels – they speak of dark weather and cold. They sing of time. They are particularly solemn in the rain.

This morning, the sea is flat and glassy as a mirror. A lone black duck cruises along, leaving its wake. When I stand still, I can hear the faint lapping of the rising tide and the *pat-pat-pat* of raindrops.

A fishing boat moves out into the distance, away from shore. Where is it going? And for how long? What dangers lie in its path?

Almost from nowhere a thunderstorm materializes, unusual in the morning. It approaches fast. First I hear the rumbles and then I can see the flashes of light in a dark cloud – the ubiquitous energy of life in a visible form. I book it for home.

Today the soundscape is especially rich, with the far-off undulating and recurrent rumble of thunder, the intermittent pattering of raindrops, the rushing of the brook, the foghorn, and the bell. Set in this backdrop, the breath is cast as a diamond on velvet. Giving myself over to gravity, I sink into the mat and die to everything outside of the moment.

I am beginning to understand that death is not just something that occurs at the end of life. Most of our adult lives are spent in an all-consuming process of building – building relationships, homes, families, careers. But for some of us something begins to happen, perhaps around the age of fifty. It starts first in response to an urge to get rid of clutter. Spaces open up and light enters in. Disposing of things becomes more pleasurable than gathering them. After a time, stripping down can grow into a yearly ritual. More time passes and more letting go, dying to agendum, to control – of other people's lives, of even our own.

For me, this process has been joyful. As the burden has lifted, my step has become lighter. As I get rid of baggage in my personal life, relationships grow smoother and less complicated. Life becomes less serious. Free. I am growing free.

Most recent to go has been what was for me the straightjacket of religiosity. I have been dying for a long time. Once letting go became an operative mode of living, it had a far-reaching effect. Like everything else in my life, religious notion has lightened up. So, here I am, floundering about with nothing solid to hang on to. Just an amorphous relationship with this something that I can neither define nor name.

~

I went into town to have a late lunch and a swim, and to spend some time at City Market. What a magnificent building. The ceiling is constructed in the form of an inverted ship's hull, so much in keeping with the sea-orientation of this Maritime province. I purchased a luscious spinach salad with all the fixings at the Wild Carrot. I ate slowly, savoring every mouthful.

After a swim at the Aquatic Center, I spent the afternoon lolling in the steam room, the sauna, and the hot tub. Such luxury. I struck up conversations with friendly locals, all of us enjoying the creature comforts of this wonderful place.

When I left the locker room to go swimming, I forgot a quarter on the bench. There were many people there, including large numbers of teens and children. I was gone for close to two hours. The quarter was still there when I returned. In a similar incident, I left a pile of change on a shelf by a pay phone. In the late afternoon, when I went back to the phone to finish my calls, the money was untouched.

~

Back at the Dipper, looking out a window toward the north, I ponder that this is the kind of day for which the word 'dreary' was invented. The scene is lush green and grey. Rain drips from the roof. From the porch I watch the raindrops on the pond – tiny concentric circles expanding into one another and disappearing as they intersect. A banjo frog croaks, as the bell buoy rings out its one-note song – a lovely sound in the rain.

The clouds break up as I settle into my sleeping bag. A breeze begins to stir, moving the surface of the pond in a patternless array of subtle ripples. Nights are precious. I make them long, retiring early and waking early, watching through the dawn.

Day 13

Sleeping on the porch, I awake several times each night to watch and listen. I have become attentive to the onset of change. The first movement of air. The arrow-like bullet of wind. The first sound of the bell buoy and foghorn. Some primitive spirit that has long been in gestation within me is being born here – soaked in fog, rising on tides. I am awash in the night. I have been cast in.

As I prepare to rise, something glistens in the morning brightness. I see a tiny web inside the screen. The spider proceeds painstakingly, slowly and exactingly. The filament emerges from her body as she narrows the concentric circles to a point. The point where she will sit – and watch and wait. Perhaps my being here closes a circle of sorts. The place, the activity, the turning of the world is complete within itself, yet is not something added by the presence of an enchanted observer?

There is a Scriptural story of Martha and Mary. It seems that Jesus came to a feast. Martha ran all about, making preparations. Mary reclined at the feet of Jesus. The story ends: "Mary has chosen the better part for herself, and it shall not be taken from her."

Drawn to the beach by that clean sea smell, I am up and out by 7 A.M. Fundy is totally flat. The only sound is a *G-lump, G-lump* of water against stone as the tide moves in. A loon emerges from a rockbound pool, rounding a corner below me and trailing a wishbone wake. Loons are solitary birds. Perhaps the call of a loon is so compelling because it is almost always superimposed on a backdrop of silence.

It is Saturday, and lots of folks are in the area for the weekend. Alice and Richard are here with their two grandchildren. Torie, her husband Scott, their children, and their dog Check are camping on their land. They have a wonderful outdoorsy family life.

Ivan and Gwen are working on preparations for their camp. Ivan is building the cabin by himself. Elizabeth stopped to chat for a bit. She has a chair on top of her waterfront knoll, where she comes to sit and de-stress. Construction of Douglas and Lorri's year-round home is coming along nicely.

Daisies are everywhere. Nell's Mother, whom I met the other day, speaks of them as "Nature's little bouquets – arranged all about to greet us." Kathy was told that Emma would come to her in daisies.

Growing wild and free, they are my favorite flower.

This afternoon, I stretched out my body on the beach for a bit, then ambled up to the far trail through the woods. I have never been able to follow this path its length without boots, as it has always been too wet. This summer, moose tracks are baked in like the imprint of some kind of prehistoric monster. This guy was no Bambi.

I had my latest soup for dinner – a stir-fry of shredded cabbage, onion, green pepper, celery, cauliflower, and bulk tomato in a yellow miso and lemon stock. Scrumptious!

Day 14

It was a chilly night, but I was toasty warm in my sleeping bag. This morning, as I lay on the porch basking in the sun, the light from the pond creates shiny reflected currents that move across the ceiling, first one way and then another – sometimes bursting in all directions from a central point.

Again I start the day in quiet meditation. Constant, steady – the breath swings back and forth. Lying face up, I dissolve into the floor.

Later, on my way to Quaker Meeting in St. Andrews, I stop at one of my favorite spots, the Blueberry Patch, a small local highway business on Route 1 that sells all kinds of things prepared from blueberries. It seems that the climate and terrain up here are well-suited to this, my favorite fruit. The little place has a staff of middle-age women in aprons who bake fresh pies and tarts. They also offer shortcake with real whipped cream and homemade baking soda biscuits. I pick up a much-appreciated pie for my Quaker friends.

I must admit that I really look forward to Quaker worship. There is something very sacred about sitting with others in gathered silence. My contemplative spirit takes over, and the hour flies by. After Meeting, we socialize, chatting about local life and political issues. These folks get involved, much the same as my home group from the Cape.

On the way back to the Dipper, I decide to explore a bit. I stop at New River Beach, a Provincial Park. Programs and festival days are held throughout the summer at this beautiful sandy beach and campground. I also visit Lepreau Falls, another Provincial Park. There are picnic tables and viewing platforms over a large river with a series of waterfalls.

Turning off into Little Lepreau, I drive by the old covered bridge, and then swing around through the small waterfront village of Maces Bay. The more that I see, the more I come to realize that coastal New Brunswick is an undiscovered treasure.

Back at the Dipper, the fragrance of Torie and Scott's campfire flavors the night air. Last night I saw another porcupine. Like skunks, they don't move very fast. They don't need to.

Day 15

I love to lie on the porch in the morning till the sun breaks over the ledge, and then throw off my sleeping bag and bask in the warmth, stretching out the full length of my body. No phone. No work. No errands or lists. The whole day lies before me, open as a new book.

I had a wake-up call last night. I can't get through my regular exercises without nerve pain in my back. I need to reappraise my activities. Long sessions of reading or writing are out, as sitting seems to aggravate the condition. I called the Clinic and made an appointment with my doctor for the day when I will be traveling back home through Boston, but there are over four weeks before then.

I attempted meditation. My practice has fallen away during the very busy spring season on the Cape. Lately, I have occasionally been slipping into a familiar state, which goes back to a time long ago. I recall sitting on a beach chair and reading *The Cloud of the Unknowing*, an old Christian classic, as the tide rose slowly around me. That was in 1981. Actually, it goes back even further – to a time as a child when I lay in the grass, peering up into the sky through the leaves.

This state was identified as contemplation by my readings in the Christian mystic tradition. I found and still find this term misleading, as it implies some object of attention. In actual fact, at least for me, this state is a point of stillness where the mind shuts off. It is not meditation, although it can occur when meditating. It is a condition of single-pointed energy. I am not thinking of the breath. I am not thinking at all. Awake and alert, I am all attention, but there is no particular object of focus. I am at rest and in a state of peace.

I cannot enter this state by any effort of my own. I can only make myself open and available to it. Sometimes it happens when I am in the presence of beauty. Or it can happen in the silence of the Quaker Meeting House. For me, it is prayer. It is identified and experienced in all the major religions, as well as by Agnostics. Throughout my years of doubting and rejecting, my contemplative experience has been a consistent source of acknowledgment that there is some channel, some personal link with the energy of the universe.

The rocks on the porch are fascinating. The energy of the wind, the trees, the sea, the little snake that suns himself beside my stoop – they hold that same pervasive energy albeit in a different way. All interconnected, as am I, the observer.

Tonight there is the wonderful fragrance of all things green. The night is still. Through the trees I see the lights of a fishing boat coming in, surrounded by screeching gulls. Mosquitoes are gathering on the screen. Silently, a cruising dragonfly snatches them up one by one. The stars emerge in the darkening sky. I slide slowly and luxuriantly into sleep.

Day 16

Something is stirring. Air movements are erratic. Foghorns converse far off in dissonant tones. A front of some sort is rising, but has yet to materialize. Change is in the air.

Today, I am uneasy. Today, change is disquieting and is accompanied by a foreboding of sorts. My mind drifts off to the children – my grandchildren, Torie and Scott's little girls, children everywhere. There are changes occurring in the weather patterns of the world that are disconcerting.

The people of Europe experienced some of the coldest weather on record last year. Temperatures in the States are going through the roof this summer. The hurricane season now extends almost into the winter. Tornados are occurring earlier every year and in unlikely places. Robins have been sighted in Alaska. It occurs to me that our behavior on this planet is causing trouble. I am put in mind of the prophetic words of Chief Seattle: "Whatever happens to the earth, happens to the sons and daughters of the earth."

It would seem that people need to pay attention. But if there is anything that I have learned in my life, it is that we cannot change things by forcing our will upon others. We can only light our own candle and hope that the flame shines true.

I awoke this morning to the sounds of red squirrels – picking, grinding, and scratching – as they survey the prospects of a food source or a nest in some nook or cranny of the Dipper. One floats over the screen on the porch as it if were gliding down a greased skid.

I was greeted on my front stoop this morning by another snowshoe hare. They are very plentiful here. My friend Patty traps them and carts them off somewhere, as they wreak havoc in her vegetable garden. I suggest that she bring them here and I will take them in. I have seen or heard no evidence of coyotes, although people say that they are around. They must be very fat, as these are big, healthy bunnies.

The tall grass is flaxen today, waving silently in the bright morning sun. There are several patches of lupin around the Dipper. These are beautiful midsummer wildflowers. How very lovely, and I didn't even have to plant them. After all the years of sowing, weeding, trimming, and seeding, I am beginning to believe that the best landscaping happens naturally, and, best of all, it is always a surprise.

Toward midday, I set out on a long morning walk on the main road. There was some traffic, mostly fishermen heading to or from work. Everybody waves to me as they pass by. Even in cars, folks around here do not fail to acknowledge one another.

Passing a yard full of lobster traps, I met a man going to his mailbox who introduced himself as Doug. We talked for a time, particularly about the occupation of fishing. Doug is the husband of Lynn, who came to the door and invited me to stop in and visit. Just some more of this uncommon Maritime hospitality.

~

After dinner I turned on the radio for some diversion and was broadsided by a heart-rending ballad. Although I could not understand the meaning of the French lyrics, I recognized in an instant the universal message imparted by the melody and the sensitive performance. It was a song of tragic loss. In the solitude of my tiny cabin, "Evangeline" ripped into my heart.

I remembered Daddy. His neatly trimmed mustache. His strong hand holding mine.

At first it was an ache in my throat – a heaving of my shoulders. And then deep, doleful bellows from the pit of my stomach, sounds I could hardly recognize as coming from me.

Emma. My dying grandbaby – breaking apart piece by piece.

I caught my breath. It began again, sliding into a groan. I think of Kathy – my poor Kathy. The purging continued . . . a catalyst for all the losses of my life.

The loss of my illusions, and especially the loss of the chance to have been a better parent for those little children of long ago. I cried as if it would never stop. Layer upon layer of loss.

Lost opportunities. Lost words. The lost music of my father.

All the nevers, as in "I'll never see him again." The pain experienced by my grown children – absorbed over and over.

The future losses. My mother. My friends.

The endings. The endings of the trips, the visits, the family gatherings. The end of my life.

I fell into the chair – exhausted.

The fog moved in from west to east, passing down the street in bundles, like ghosts on parade.

Day 17

I awake at 2 A.M. All is still. I listen for a sound – any sound – but there is nothing. Not even a whisper of a breeze. And then, from far off shore, the horn of a ship. Low and mournful. Repeating every thirty seconds or so. Moving off in the distance. Moving away. I listen, wondering about its port of origin and the lives of those on board. I listen – and then it is gone. Passing through like my passing sorrow. A loon calls close off shore. One cry – nothing more.

I feel a change in the air. A cool, damp bite on my face. The first few drops make tiny splashes on the pond. Rain. It is to be a day of rain. The boat, the solitary loon, the rain – a fitting coda for "Evangeline" – and the long grief.

Assembling ingredients, I start the day by nurturing myself with some homemade soup. I have invented a new recipe. First I sauté onions and garlic, then folding in bulk tomatoes and the juice in which they are packed. Then I add water, lentils, broccoli, sweet potatoes, kale, a few carrots, and some brown rice. When it is ready to eat, I stir in some yellow miso and lemon juice. The Dipper steeps in warm, delicious food smells in this dark and wet weather.

Settling in to read, I pick up *Faith and Practice of the New England Yearly Meeting of Friends*, a book of Quaker readings, and *Plain Living: A Quaker Path to Simplicity* by Catherine Whitmire. For the most part, I am in accord with Quaker principles, and, as far as I know, there is no core of dogma to which I must concede. Today I am feeding myself with soup, and simple, solid, reasonable thought.

It is windy. The pond, which so sensitively reflects even the subtlest changes, is in a state of frenetic motion. The rain pelts the cabin, as I let go into the night.

Day 18

It is a grey morning. The foghorn sounds in the distance. Sadness returns as the fog rolls in. Today it is a quiet sadness. Unattached. A feeling only – a broad, sweeping feeling. I let it wash over me as I settle in my chair . . . breathing in . . . breathing out . . . .

A shore bird has chosen my pond to feed. A dauber, he tilts his entire body up and down, back and forth, as he forages for food, with an occasional wild strike at the frog.

The red squirrels have returned, digging and probing. They are determined. They are industrious. They are a problem. At my first stirrings they cease, but resume their activity when I become quiet. Assuming an aggressive posture, one confronts me, sassing brazenly when I open the door. They seem bolder and larger and more resourceful than their Wellfleet cousins.

A baby bunny seems to be residing under my stoop. She scampers off when I step outside, but she doesn't go far. She greets me when I return from my walk. We observe each other for some time. At length, we converse. I talk. She wiggles her nose. I tell her that she is safe here – and welcome. She speaks of the tender green grasses and the carrot peels that she finds in the compost pile.

I caught some morning programming on the radio, as I attempted gentle stretches prior to a walk. News from the States on relaxed environmental controls was upsetting. Power plants are no longer required to cap their greenhouse gas emissions, nor do they have to upgrade their facilities in order to conform to previous environmental standards. I promise myself that I won't rant about this as I am wont to do time and time again. But there's Sydney . . . and Kendall and Alyssa . . . and Derrick and Mark . . . and the big kids – and now little Julia. They are the ones who will inherit this situation that they had no part in creating.

I feel the onslaught of a thought attack.

I have signed on for Green Power and I am planning to buy a hybrid car. I have propane heat, which I keep at a very low setting. I recycle. I turn out any lights that I am not using. Short of carrying a sign, which I might do at some time, I don't know how else to do my part. I think of Craig, my grandson. He shares many of my values, and, for a teenager, he is unusually attuned to the implications of disregard for the environment. We are going to need more young adults like him.

I walk to the beach, climb on the rocks, and reflect on the solidness of the cliffs that bind the coast of New Brunswick. Solid – like the people who live and work here.

By the end of the day, the Dipper had once again done its work. As I slid into my sleeping bag, a frog hopped into the pond. A bell buoy sounded, and then a distant foghorn. I lay on my back motionless. The subtlest possible draft of air touches my face.

I drift off to sleep.

Day 19

This morning, as I begin my walk, I am greeted by an orange butterfly. It emerges from the brush, passes in front of me, and marks the path ahead before flying off. I walk to the white cliffs and sit for a long time, looking out over Fundy.

The pointed firs rise in relief against the fog, spectral and still. All different sizes and shapes, their contours and dimensions are formed by the elements in which they live. Some are full and healthy. Some are scrawny and whipped. Some have no branches at all, save for a cluster near the top. Some are alone, while others grow in deep, dark groves, their new growth thrust upward to the light. Some appear as if in layers, the closer ones more distinct. Those further away – faint and filmy silhouettes – fade into the mist, surrendered. At every turn, I meet them. At every turn.

Needing some special groceries, I go to the Whole Food Store in St. George. Reminiscent of my favorite store on Cape Cod, an establishment of the same name in Orleans, the place even smells the same.

On the way back to the Dipper, I listen to the radio in the car. On a call-in show, the question is presented: "Are you enjoying your vacation and is it doing what it should for you?" It appears that many people keep their cell phones active, some visit Internet Cafes, and some even bring work along. The host suggests leaving everything behind and dealing with it when the vacation is over. For a brief moment, I think of what a backlogged mess my prolonged absence will engender. Then I quickly call to mind Eastern principles and the pointed firs, surrender to it, and let go into the present moment.

Sundown is late here, as New Brunswick is on the edge of the Atlantic Time Zone. Tonight it is warm, clear, and still. The pond is like a sheet of indigo glass, reflecting the ledge and a small grove of birch trees. The gently rolling sea provides an audio backdrop for the end of this summer day.

Day 20

Awakening in the wee small hours of the morning, I open my eyes and ears to the drama of the night. A meteor flies across the horizon. The slightest trace of diesel oil is in the air. It comes. It goes. A reminder of the people who are working here. A star twinkles through the crown of a birch tree. Weird animal sounds move through the woods – close.

Pain darts down the back of my right leg. Fleeting. Quick. I observe its passing – and, once again, sink into sleep.

Arising at dawn, I take a crisp and cool morning walk. The change of seasons begins early in the northern forest. As I pass along the path, I am drawn to the pointed firs. They have become a living presence to me. Companions. Today I am drawn to their tiny shoots – closest to the light.

I walk on. There is a new fragrance in the air this morning, like nothing that I have ever smelled before. Spruce – yes! – and salt, but also this other indescribable something. Light. Fresh. Clean. Just slightly sweet. It does not come and go as other fragrances, but stays constant throughout my walk.

Day 21

It was cold through the night. This morning I loll around in the sack for a long time. Sunrise breaks suddenly, and, in an instant, it is day. I watch the brilliant sunshine move across the rocks on the porch, highlighting first one facet and then another with sharp lines of contrast between light and shadow.

I choose one and pick it up. It is still cold with night. The sun moves down my body. I feel its warmth take my shoulders and then my hips and thighs. How very fast it moves.

Pain radiates from my back into my right leg. It throbs and pulsates. I lie with it and feel its nuances and subtleties. It is not unlike a current of sorts. Erratic pulsations and then moments of absence. After a time there is the pain and there is the watcher. Not me and my pain, but me and *the* pain. As the discomfort subsides and migrates to my foot for a last flourish, I return to the breath, rising and falling with the gentle breeze.

The rock, a pretty grey heart shape with white stripes of varying width and angle, has a single thin vertical line that intersects the horizontal markings on both sides, a reminder for me once again this morning of impermanence. As surely as the shadow of this pen is shortening, everything is changing – moving into new dimensions and configurations – and I am swept along with it. I hold the rock in my hand. It warms to my body.

The sun is now full on my face. This short time has marked

the movement of the planet. It goes through its routine silently and dependably, as the drama of human life swirls about on its surface, heedless of the daily miracle that is taking place. And it is all of one piece, connected by the rhythms, the gesticulations, the very pulsation and throbbing itself.

We are all trapped here. All of us and everything. All nourished by the same finite sources. All infused with the same basic energy. We humans have the unique ability to observe and reflect. Sometimes, I think that is our most sublime purpose.

I roll over. The sun warms me down to my bones. The air is light and dry and slightly moving. It wafts over my face and hands. There is the nagging thought that I must get up and get going. I observe this, and let it go with the breath. This is unfamiliar territory – this long rest and respite.

The breath can be fascinating. Lying on my back, I can ride the rise and fall . . . over and over . . . again and again . . . .

There is a strong early-fall breeze. In the slanted light of dawn, even the tiny rocks cast shadows. The shadow of my pen and fingers is fascinating – seemingly solid, and yet a phantom of no tangible substance. I play with it, composing designs of light and dark, manipulating angles and shapes.

A single strand of hair falls before my eyes. It shines silver in the sun.

~

I am up at 9 A.M. and off to Quaker Meeting in St. Andrews. My friends, as always, are warm and welcoming. We gather around in a circle near the windows. Light pours in. I am bathed in it. The sun on the old wood of the studio loft creates a sense of solidness. The friendly wear of many seasons shines brightly. Folks speak today, mostly about the world situation. I slip into contemplative prayer, sitting silently, infused by something – who can say? The same energy? The same ubiquitous energy? This feels like worship to me. And it feels good. And it feels right.

We gather at Julie's house for an unplanned lunch and some tea. Folks whip something together quickly and easily. I love these people. Like the UUs, they are down-to-earth and real.

I spent a little time in St. Andrews, a quaint and touristy kind of town with a huge castle-like hotel on a hill overlooking the village and the bay. Walking the streets, I enjoyed a couple of hours of leisurely browsing. Merchants seem to take pride in maintaining the ambience of a welcoming and inviting main street. Although I am not a shopper, this is a real treat when I have nothing else to do.

Day 22

I have a full day ahead with errands in town and I am tempted to skip my morning meditation, but I realize that the practice is what gives the retreat its fullness. I lay on my sleeping bag on the porch in the morning sun. I feel the warmth on my back and I settle down. Long, deep breaths.

The dragonflies make their electric *click-clack* as they cruise the pond for insects. Intermittently, I hear the motor of a fishing boat. A frog croaks. Thoughts intrude. Breathing in . . . breathing out . . . I touch them lightly and let them go, even the powerful and compelling ones. Surrendering my body to gravity, I die into the mat on the floor.

~

Later in the morning, I go to Saint John to pick up the results of the well water test. Everything looks fine. I have lunch at the Thai Hut, a little restaurant on the hill in the business district, and enjoy Pad Thai for the second time in my life.

Walking the streets a bit, I pause for a while on the harbor front. I have always been drawn to ships and docks. Perhaps this is some kind of a cellular memory extending back to the turn of the twentieth century and to Wisconsin, where my grandfather owned and operated a combination freight and passenger boat.

My father's fondest memories were of summers spent on Lake Michigan, going to work with his Dad. He told of storms and the antics of deck hands, of how his father would lower him over the side, tethered by a rope. His father died when he was ten, and the boat was sold.

There is a theory that a sense of place is embedded deep in the psyche of a young child. When Dad came east as a young man, he left his heart behind on the waters of his youth. I remember the fisherman and his son coming ashore from the fishing boat in Dipper Harbour, and wonder if people with boats and water in their background can ever really leave.

At Kings Square, old folks are enjoying the beautiful day. There is a Pensioners Home adjacent to this lovely green area. What a great spot for seniors – just a few steps from the bank, shops, and City Market.

Back at the Dipper, I lay down to meditate. I can smell a wood fire. Its fragrance is rich and mellow. Like only the sense of smell can do, it takes me back – way back. To the Andersons' camp when I was eight years old . . . to Dighton, Massachusetts, and our wood burning furnace . . . to campsites with my children.

A heron squawks close by. Fog rolls in. I inhale. I let go. Fog turns to sun and back to fog and then blends into a sunset.

Just before I go to bed, I hear a noise outside and wonder if it is my little friend. I slowly approach the window to see not only my special baby but also her brother and mother, all munching on my yard. Even when I open the door, they appear to be calm and comfortable. They allow me to move out onto the stoop, and do not run away. The mother is as big as my favorite cat Chloe, and the babies are the size of the adult rabbits of the Cape.

I stand there for a long time, feeling like Jane Goodall with her chimps. There is something about the presence of animals browsing and eating that evokes peace and serenity. These bunnies surely do it for me.

During the night, a much needed soaking summer rain moved in. I lay sleepless for a bit and listened to the raindrops on the pond, the thunder rolling back and forth in the distance across the bay, and the foghorn cutting through the weather.

Day 23

I awake at 4 A.M. It has been a dark night. The pointed firs form a black fringe for the sky. Foghorns converse against the muffled surf. One low, long and deep; the other, higher and more urgent. A bell buoy sounds – firm and solid. I imagine rust. The lights of a fishing boat pass by, headed out so very early in the morning. I lay my fragile presence against this living landscape. Slipping off like the boat, I fall back into sleep. Borne by time, I float through into another day.

The rain begins early in the morning. It is like a symphony, with tone, cadence, and volume – at first hushed and gentle, then with power and force. I wonder where the baby bunnies are.

I watch my monkey mind flitting here and there. The future. The past. Things to do when I return home. Plans. I can drown in plans. I am two people. The one who lies here on the porch listening to the rain, and the other one – the one who is everywhere, anywhere except in the present moment.

A red squirrel announces its presence. I must get up and set the trap. At the Dipper, bunnies are surely more welcome than red squirrels.

After a hearty breakfast of rice cereal, mixed nuts, pumpkin and sunflower seeds, and dried cranberries – all in oat milk – I decide to dress for rain and attempt a walk. On the way back to the cabin, I once again stand amongst the pointed firs. In the darkness of the grove their wood is covered with lichen, their dead branches hang with moss. Their life passes upward, surrendered to the light. Adapting day by day, they are shaped by forces not of their making.

I come upon the pointed fir that stands alone in the meadow, looking out over the sea. I imagine it in a storm. The Fundy gales are powerful. It is in a dangerous spot. It did not choose its place, but, because others do not surround it, light reaches all of its branches.

I walk on, the mist in my face. The gift of the Little Dipper is for today only. I can know nothing of tomorrow. I can plan. I can even obsess. But all is change. And the pointed firs know well of that.

Day 24

As I rise to go on an extended walk, I pause to look around the cabin. The simplicity is elegant. I remember the words of Thoreau: "... a man is rich in proportion to the number of things that he can afford to let alone...."[2]

This morning I walked the main road toward the next village, pausing along the way to look at the two peninsulas that extend into the cove. One is solid rock with perhaps five or six trees. The other is lined with pointed firs, which create a ragged ridge across the top. The sea is still, and colored in layered shades of grey-blue like the sky. I cannot describe how barren and desolate the place appears. What is it about the northern coastline that speaks to me so strongly? What is it about the living stillness? And whereof the mysterious connection that I find here?

On my walk, thoughts of my other life keep intruding. Mind racing takes me over. Clients. Problems. The pile of mail that will await me, each piece requiring some response. Catch-up marketing, errands and medical visits for Mom and me, and possible physical therapy for my back. Phone calls – and more phone calls. Fall projects around the house that must be done and food prep for the freezer. I feel the contraction of another thought attack.

I remember to watch the thinker. These things are not my life. There are birds on the Cape. There is fog and rain and the fragrance of the sea and even coyote songs in the night, if I simply remember to be there. It is my mind that causes me trouble. It is how I process my life.

The Fundy tide is rolling in. Migratory birds dart back and forth over the marsh. By the wayside there is a stinging nettle bush, a tangle of sweet peas, and a small stand of some type of wildflower with yellow blossoms on delicate stems. Lupin is everywhere. Colors are more vibrant on this dark day. I disturb an otter as I stop to look. We pause for a moment and regard each other before he disappears into the brush.

Back at the Dipper, there is a wildflower along the pond edge with tiny blossoms that look like miniature orchids. It grows on a delicate maroon stem, and is similar to the alpine flower that is found on the tops of the five thousand foot White Mountains of New Hampshire.

The wildflowers around the Dipper will be more abundant every year, as the land makes its comeback from the logging operation. There is a particularly eye-catching patch in my front yard. Asters. Goldenrod. Daisies. The flowers are tightly crammed together, but still blossom wildly. The ledge is bordered by piles of decaying slash, with new life emerging from every crevice and cranny. Healing! Resurrection! The place is being reborn.

I lay down in the sun. The warmth through my clothing feels healthy and life giving. A bee is busy pollinating some wild flowers and is totally uninterested in me. The flowers themselves are fascinating – multiple spires with tiny balls on the end, all attached to a central sphere. They look like miniature communication satellites. As I extend my gaze, I see many of them, all awash in bees.

The whole scene – the sun, the bees, the flowers, the tiny ferns and wooded plants, the slash, me – all connected by this same current, this same energy. How to tell of it? How to name it? How?

The fog rolls in as the day draws to a close, and tonight I am visited by a tiny baby bunny. Anyone who might happen by would think that I talk to myself.

Day 25

Restless night. I haven't a clue as to why. Leaves twitch as trees stand alert. The forest waits in anticipation – poised – present to the new day.

Morning meditation is disjointed, with my mind racing all over the place. I finally resort to counting my breaths and allowing my breathing to become shallow. Little breaths of the cool, delicious morning air.

This morning, I walk to the boundary of my land and on into the woods. At first there is one tiny butterfly. And then, in a flurry, butterflies materialize all around me. I stand amongst them, these winged bearers of grace.

On a trip to the White Mountains shortly after Emma's death, I experienced my first butterfly encounter. I remember bending down to tighten the laces of my boots as I prepared to climb Mount Washington. Initiating a visit, an orange butterfly landed on my bare leg.

Compassionate Friends is a large self-help organization for families of deceased children, composed of bereaved parents, siblings, and grandparents. Their symbol is the butterfly. During the years following Emma's death, my daughter Kathy cried herself well at Compassionate Friends meetings.

Their yearly national convention hosts over a thousand people.

I have never attended a more moving event. Some people have lost more than one child. One individual lost three children in separate automobile accidents.

Walls and bulletin boards display photos of deceased children, complete with mementos, descriptions of the children's accomplishments, and explanations of the Foundations, Scholarships, and other such things established in the children's names. At the last convention, which was particularly large, I stood in the presence of all that pain, overwhelmed.

Yet people have hope. And, after a time, they give back to others. The entire horrible experience seems to engender deep compassion. Those who don't flee the pain, but go through it, become a whole new creation.

I walk away the day. The pointed firs catch my eye. The tiny shoots, closest to the light. *Look up! Look up!*

Returning to the cabin, I sit by the pond. The dragonflies have taken over. A particularly large pink species seems to have the ability to hover, poised in mid-air like a helicopter.

Day 26

Another restless night. I lay sleepless from about 2 A.M. on. I noticed that the moon was just off full. There are times when this affects me. I become hyper-alert and have trouble sleeping, almost as if I have had caffeinated coffee. I see this "full moon syndrome," as I refer to it, in other people. There is no scientific basis for it, but I am convinced that it exists.

Shortly after 5 A.M., I got up, went into the house, and turned on the radio. During the night, CBC runs programming from other countries around the world. I listened to Radio Australia. On the way back to Wellfleet the last time that I was here, Radio Poland was broadcast. At another time I heard broadcasting from Germany. Everything is presented in English, which is rapidly becoming the universal language. I read in some piece of Canadian literature that foreign countries are now teaching academic subjects in English.

In the morning, I went to the nearest convenience store, several miles away in Lepreau. I stopped at the docks in Dipper Harbour and sat in the car for a time, reflecting upon how much substance there is in this little town and all the other fishing villages along the New Brunswick coast.

I stopped back at the abandoned house at the end of the cove. The door was open, so I went in.

Old. Basic. Bright. A simple structure carved out of a strangely beckoning, hard and rough landscape. There are small bedrooms, a kitchen, and a common room. A wood stove seems to have been the only heat source. The front porch looks out over a large cove. No other dwelling can be seen from this homestead, which is about a half mile in from the main road. The place is totally simple, but probably more luxurious than most people in the world can ever hope to have.

In the afternoon, I visited Patty and Bill's. Always welcoming and hospitable, they put on the teakettle and brought out the cookies. Bill told me that he had grown up in the little house, along with five siblings and his parents. He said that the winters were cold (I can only imagine!), and that he and his siblings had to walk the two-and-a-half miles to school and back again every day. If they balked because of the weather, his father would take down an alder switch from the wall. That was all that was necessary to get them going. He told of feeling deprived because he had lobster sandwiches (lobster was abundant here), and the other kids had peanut butter. The three babies in the grave are his siblings. He related that lots of babies and small children died before they even got to school.

Bill also told of the death of his father when he was fifteen years old, followed three months later by the death of his only sister at the age of fifteen to polio. I cannot imagine how his mother endured the gut-wrenching pain she faced in her lifetime.

Coming back along the cliffs, I paused for a moment. A seal swam and dove off the rocks. There is a salmon farm a short distance away. Almost every time that I come here, it is being worked by at least two fishing boats. The operation is somewhat noisy. On some days, the diesel smell overpowers the smell of the sea.

Folks with property along the shore are protesting. Like everything else, there are two sides to this. I am told that the Atlantic species of salmon is almost extinct, and that fish farms are the only way to provide them to a salmon-hungry public. I am also told that no one knows as of yet whether the run-off from feed, medicine, and excrement will be a pollutant for the surrounding area.

There is a circular dilemma here. Salmon are over-fished. Eventually, the supply of salmon runs out. A new way for everyone to have all the salmon that they desire is created, but this is undertaken without the approval of a small number of people whose lives will be affected. Has no one thought of perhaps eating less salmon?

Is this not parallel to the current situation with oil – and forests – and arable farmland – and all of our other natural resources? Whoever said that we should be able to have all that we want of everything that we like? We are using things up at the peril of the small number of people who are immediately adversely affected, and ultimately at our own. Them is us. Less is more.

I believe that there is a principle of balance that needs to be considered in this and in so many other situations of dissonance and stalemate. Both sides can be partially right. And both sides can be partially wrong. And there is always a better way, but it takes both sides together to find it.

I took a ride out Cranberry Head Road to a beautiful cove, so typically New Brunswick, and then to Chance Harbour. Today the tide was very low.

"Fundy Fishermen Days" begins this evening with Bingo at the Fire Station. This is a yearly celebration and a big event for folks from Dipper Harbour and the surrounding communities.

Day 27

I awoke in eager anticipation of the day ahead. The kick-off was a pancake breakfast at the Fundy Bay Senior Center in nearby Maces Bay. When I arrived at 8 A.M., the place was full, with a line out into the parking lot.

Betty and Lars, my UU friends, were there with Lena, a little girl from Belarus who is staying with them for the summer. She comes from the area of Chernobyl, the site of the Russian nuclear disaster. Some New Brunswick families are hosting children for a summer getaway from this understandably depressed place. Lena is a beautiful child. She sat quietly, clutching her bear, a stuffed animal from home that she has virtually not put down since she arrived. Lars and Betty have clearly fallen in love with her.

The breakfast was a classic hometown affair. Hosts included adolescents and old folks, with a slew of people, including men in aprons, pitching in with the cooking and cleaning up. Next came a giant yard sale, held indoors at the fire station because of the threat of rain. Unable to resist a bargain, I made some purchases for the grandchildren.

The local firemen were much in evidence, in charge of seeing to it that the traffic kept flowing in and out of the village. Available parking was limited, especially as the weather began to clear and the crowd began to gather.

The opening ceremony was in the village. The crew of a fishing boat that was lost at sea was honored. Death is an omnipresent reality in the lives of these people. I felt the universal ache of loss. Since Emma, I know that there is no way to make it better.

The day of fun then began. There were dory races with local contestants, cheered on by their families and friends. Later in the day there was a scallop-shucking contest. This drew a really big crowd.

For the children, there was a clown, a face painter, a plastic inflatable bouncing platform, a magician, an over-sized and friendly "lobster" handing out candy, and a contraption with a man in a chair who was to be submerged in water when participants hit a target with a ball. There was much enthusiasm expressed at the prospect of dunking this good-natured guy.

The New Brunswick Seafood Association was represented. Smoked herring and other such treats were given away. The Canadian Coast Guard was on hand, offering a tour of a Coast Guard vessel. The Nuclear Waste Management Organization was also present. They are seeking input from Canadians on the issue of the disposal of spent fuel from nuclear power plants. I picked up a packet composed of printed literature and a DVD.

I bought a walking stick that was handcrafted by a local teenager, Colton, the nephew of my carpenter. I complimented him on his ingenuity and enterprise, and he noted that the stick that I chose was perfect for my height and grasp.

Colton's mother had an adjoining booth. She sold bags of dulse, a form of seaweed. I bought some to try in my soup.

There was a long line at the chowder and fish cake booth. The cook was a retired fireman and the brother of my carpenter. I went back for seconds. It was a sell-out shortly after 1 P.M.

I sat on a bench and people-watched, thoroughly enjoying the beautiful weather and the hometown feeling. Folks were animated and joyful, but I have the impression that life does not necessarily come easy here, that people are good at making do, that community bonding is strong, and that roots go deep.

Then came my favorite event – the lobster crate races. This has to be planned to coincide with the high tide, which this year was near mid-day. A big crowd gathered on the beach as lobster traps were strung together with rope, extending from the dock out to a float. Both adults and children were invited to attempt to traverse the course.

There was a lot of interest, as money prizes were awarded. Folks of all ages, sizes, and shapes participated. Falls were the order of the day, and it quickly became apparent that, the lighter and more agile the contestant, the better the prospects.

Some large adults were quickly eliminated, making it only to the third or fourth crate, to the laughter and appreciation of the crowd. A little girl literally glided across, hesitating on the float for a long time before coming back. The winner was a boy of perhaps eleven years of age, who exuded confidence, running back and forth with neither a slip nor a falter.

Everyone seemed to know this young man and one another at this community gathering, reminiscent of the days of my childhood.

The day was not yet over. From seven to midnight there was music and dancing on the dock. The weather was perfect. The crowd reassembled, complete with chairs, blankets, and mosquito spray. The first act blew me away. Two teenagers, Matthew Hayes and Brad Trecartin, performed on the fiddle and the keyboard. They were followed by Perry Craft, a member of the New Brunswick Country Music Hall of Fame, on the fiddle. The crowd was most appreciative, standing and clapping along. The music was similar to that of the Celtic musicians that Nicole and I enjoyed at Mabou on the Cape Breton fiddle trail.

Al and Brenda Hooper, a husband and wife duo, performed homespun country for about half an hour. I stood in the background, amazed that I was there – a senior citizen from the States – at this wonderful small-town-Canada gathering.

Back at the Dipper, I went to sleep on the porch to the far-off sound of music, happily contented with the choice of this particular place as my Walden.

Day 28

Exercising this morning, I am again drawn to regard my surroundings. The simplicity is elegant. I flourish in this simple environment. Everything that I need is here, and nothing of any essential nature is missing. In the face of a culture of more and bigger, I am downsizing to less and smaller.

I take an early morning walk to the beach. The sun has heated the rocks. I lie on the beach amongst the pebbles, with my knees up and my hat over my face. The warmth against my spine feels wonderful. I fall asleep for a time. The feeling of moisture in the air awakens me. I am enveloped in fog.

I have had much occasion to study the fog here in coastal New Brunswick. I have observed that there are at least three varieties. Type one is actually a low cloud, usually rolling in from the bay. A second version straggles in, in wisps and streamers. Type three, my special favorite, simply materializes as if from out of nowhere.

Walking home, I reflect back on the Fundy Fisherman Days celebration. The only negative moment was the sight of a behemoth S.U.V. on the side of the narrow street leading to the village, parked amongst modest sedans. It was from New York, and was the only car from the States other than my own. It was entirely out of place, and almost blocked traffic. A man emerged, and when he turned toward me, I saw on the front of his t-shirt a particularly large American flag with the words, "Proud to be an American." How *gauche*, this ambassador.

Again at sunset, I walked to the beach, and, as usual, scanned the stones for a keeper. A small, dark grey rock, speckled and heart shaped with a white band around the top, caught my eye. A big chip had been taken out of the upper right corner. This is the second off-kilter heart that I have found this trip. I placed it with other similarly shaped stones on the porch – some cracked, some broken in half, none intact. I thought of little Emma – her death – and other heart-rending events, but today none of these made the connection.

The wound in this heart – the chunk that has been lopped off – has to do with my country.

I can remember back in earlier years, when I left the States for the first time in order to visit Linda in England where she was living and working, and when I went on a subsequent trip to Yugoslavia later in the decade, wanting to kneel down and kiss the ground when I returned home. What has happened? How have my values and the cultural norm become so divergent? I don't think that I have changed. What has become of the ideals of my life that I once found represented by the standards of my country? Today it is hard to find them, except in the lives of the many individual Americans whom I respect and admire.

When I reflect upon what I feel, it is not the anger that I outwardly manifest. Instead, it is a deep and abiding sadness. How can I ever repair my heart?

Day 29

Awakening to the autumn weather, I stayed huddled in the warmth of my sleeping bag for a long time.

The rain begins gently this morning, forming tiny bubbles that ride on the pond surface for a brief moment. As I watch, an insect lands on the inside of the screen. About an inch and a half long, it looks like a gigantic mosquito or an earwig with wings. Half of its delicate body is a long needle-like appendage. I leave to do some tasks. Returning, I find that it is still there. I gently lift it with tissue paper and release it outside. I hope that it survives. It must have some function in the scheme of things.

I began the day by reading a few things that I had brought from home. Betty Ann had written of an adventure with her family, camping in a slot canyon in northern New Mexico. With a bucket, some mud, and lots of imagination, her grandson Dylan constructed rivers, lakes, waterfalls, and dams to the joy and delight of his little cousin Amelia. Grandma told him of other cliffs and waterfalls, and Dylan understood that he had created a real landscape, complete with erosion, in miniature. Betty Ann wrote:

> *I see the energy of life within the small stream. I sense the strength of life through generations, mirrored in this moment of play... Life's persistence as it wends its way through slot canyons, across the mud, over the bank, and into the ocean ... relentless, enduring, reaching.*

The clouds begin to break and the day clears. I walk to the beach. As summer moves toward autumn, the sea is changing – rising to a richer fullness. A long line of seabirds passes across the bay, flying very close to the water, infused with the same relentless and enduring persistence. I return to the Dipper to lie on the porch and meditate.

Silently I watch my breath . . . rising . . . falling . . . Surrendered into deep rest, I experience a sense of floating – of being moved along – perhaps on a river, through a slot canyon. And on some other days, meditation is just all the noise in my head.

Day 30

I awake at midnight. The moon is near full, hanging over the ledge and silhouetting the birches. It is framed by white clouds. This is the stuff of artists. Any words I have are inadequate to describe the scene.

At 4 A.M., I awake again. The moon is so bright that gazing upon it is uncomfortable for my eyes. Trees are reflected in the pond as if it were day. Two parallel birches resemble black stilts cast against pewter. The soft, muffled call of an owl rises – close. What great grace has delivered me to this place?

I look toward the ledge. By the pond it is a pile of boulders. I wonder at the journey of these massive rocks in the great glacier of long ago. Draped with moss, hung with old roots, the ledge is aglow with otherworldly light. I reflect on the silent passage of energy from sun to moon – and then between the far, cold, lighted craters and the rocks of earth. As I lift my arm, my shadow is cast upon a ledge. An arm raised against a beam of light given off by a burning sphere, intercepted and redirected by an orbiting celestial body to a rock ledge by a pond.

Rolling over to lie on my stomach, I raise up so that I can look into the meadow, all bathed in silver. I slowly sweep my eyes from left to right, back down the line of the ledge to the birches, the pond, the firs, and out toward the sea. This is worship for me in the profoundest sense.

The spell is broken by the sound of a jet – a reminder of time and man. I am sunk so deep into this place that sometimes I forget what I am.

The moon is fading. A bat flies across my line of vision. A rush of water signals the shifting of the Fundy tide. The glow subsides. The meadow slides into darkness. The magic of the night falls away into day.

Out early this morning, I seek an easy route to the white cliffs. Bushwhacking my way through the woods, I pass a small pool of water along a tiny stream, and the smell plunges me back into my childhood. As I continue on through a field, grasshoppers fly off in all directions. Grasshoppers in jars, crickets under woodpiles, fields of wild flowers, trees with low branches to climb on – these are the things that interested me when I was a little girl. This was the stuff of my passion.

My parents were urban people, but I was a cut from a different fabric. I remember only one childhood vacation when I was taken to a woodsy place. We stayed in a cabin on a small river. I learned to swim, to row a boat, and to paddle a canoe. I saw real fish, and even encountered leeches. I loved it! My parents didn't last the week.

Mom and Dad exposed me to the best of city life. I am grateful for that. I love to spend time in Boston and Manhattan, but my roots are sunk deep in the woods. And I am realizing that the woods are where I have come to heal.

I continue on my walk to the bog. I sit on a stump and ponder my time here. I am changing. I can feel it. On the way back to the cabin, I think about this morning's news and the condition of the world: the world is changing, too. Unfortunately, many of the positive changes are not widely reported.

Back on Cape Cod last spring, I took myself out for a Chinese dinner. Patrick, a young man from Nepal, was my server. We chatted for a few moments. He told me that his lifelong heroes were Ghandhi, Martin Luther King, Jr., and Abraham Lincoln. He said that he believed that all Gods were one, and that he didn't like religions that supported war. He told his version of a Bible story. He said that Adam and Eve were given two apples, but they wanted more. Soon they were taking apples that belonged to others, and then there was war. He suggested that one apple for one person seems to be a fair arrangement. How perceptive this Nepalese man in the States on a green card.

People like him seem to be cropping up all over. An army of the wise. A quiet force for sanity. When I meet them, they are usually alone, but something tells me that they are legion.

There seems to be a movement afoot. People are becoming aware of the disorder that surrounds them, the shortsightedness of public policy, and the irresponsibility of human behavior. More and more people are in favor of doing what's right for the long term rather than what is expedient and self-serving in the now.

I believe that, oftentimes, change steeps and simmers below the surface for a long while before a ground swell can be detected. I remember when folks were beginning to become aware of the dangers of smoking. Here and there, a person would quit – first a few of my friends, and then all of them. Once, when I was traveling to Vermont, I stopped at a McDonalds. A sign on the window read: "This is a smoke-free restaurant." That was the first wave of a tide of change.

Some of the folks that I most respect are suggesting that we must not lose heart, that the turmoil in the world is all part of a larger process – the preparation for the birth of a new order. Dare I to hope?

For every event there is an arising, a first inclination. I feel as if I may be watching the very first light of a new day. New shoots springing from old roots and rising up through the ground. I probably will not be here to witness, but I will be one of those who first raised an arm to the light, and that is entirely enough.

As I finish writing this, a hummingbird comes to my window, pauses, and flies away.

Day 31

I awake in the middle of the night and begin to write. Over my shoulder, the moon is lighting the paper silver-grey. Across the pond the pointed firs stand straight and still. Above them hangs a lone star. Framed by a panel on the screen, the picture evokes a strange memory. Something vestigial. Something from the primitive past. Were my roots deep in an ancient forest? Have I come here to remember?

A snowshoe hare crosses my path as I begin my morning walk. Further along, wings whirring and beating, a pheasant starts from the roadside. The fragrance of the marsh is sweet with life. Along the way, at approximately the same place every day, I hear the call of the wood thrush. Lyrical and hauntingly beautiful, it echoes through the forest. Having nothing but time and no preoccupations, I stand and listen.

Back at the cabin, I settle into my lounge chair to write in this journal. I notice a spreading darkness arising from the direction of the Bay of Fundy and a strong wind coming up quickly. I go outside to anchor small items. The rain begins. Darts of wind shoot through the screen. *P-hew! P-hew!*

And now I hear the thunder, and the flashes begin. Rain falls in torrents and rushes off the roof. Trees sway. The thunder moves closer, echoing against the cliffs and through the ledge. And now a flash and a sounding at the same instant! A strike nearby! I check to make sure that I am not touching metal in my chair. I smell the ozone. I am out of the chair and onto the mat on the floor.

The storm rumbles on for ten, maybe fifteen minutes. Lying on the floor, I feel the cabin shake with the force of it. And then it passes, moving off to the west like a massive armored ghost ship.

Day 32

On this very cool midsummer morning, I awake with my sleeping bag pulled up over my already hooded head. Peeking out, I see pink clouds covering the eastern sky. As the sun breaks the horizon, the clouds become tinged with gold, appearing as shiny fish scales. I glance at the pond to see the reflection in the dark mirror – pink baubles on black glass. In no more than three minutes, the clouds fall away.

The expanding universe intrigues me – celestial bodies moving apart from one another at enormous speeds. How vast the design. How small our little lives. How insignificant our niggling discomforts – and yet, are we not all in all? Most of the time it would seem that way.

I cannot grasp infinity. Earthbound, I know of nothing that does not have a beginning and an end. The idea that outer space just goes on and on is mind boggling to me. There must be an edge or the wall of an enormous box. There must be other worlds like ours, other forms of life. Is there a single strand that runs through thunderstorms, pink clouds, exploding supernovas, and extra-terrestrials?

I walk to the beach. A group of kayaks is passing, probably from Eastern Outdoors, a camping and excursion business from Dipper Harbour. I lie in the stones, listening to laughter and thinking of my family.

Back at the camp, I turn on the radio. It is hurricane season, and the storms in the southern U.S. are becoming more and more powerful. I believe that this is related to the human impact upon the environment.

It seems that time is becoming our enemy. Relentless, it presses on as we quibble over where to place a wind farm. Is this the year that the runaway train starts down the hill? Has it already started? Or is it to start this moment with this emission from this fossil fuel burning power plant? And where is God in all of this? It would seem that we are being called to be responsible for our own actions.

I am the eagle, the bat, the bunny. I am the oak tree outside my window in Wellfleet. I am little Julia. And my life and the lives of my progeny will be increasingly altered with each new generation because of the behavior of a single species. I apologize for my own kind. We need to change.

Day 33

The sun has made a bright appearance. There is a huge bank of white cumulus clouds against the brilliant blue sky, passing from west to east on the northern horizon. As I scurry outside for a better look, I almost step on a large green snake lazing on the rocks. I scare him. He scares me. And we both go our way.

I watch the fast-moving metamorphosis. In not more than a minute, the cauliflower top of a giant cloud flips to the side and another crown rises in its place. Two other monoliths tumble into one another. The enormous bank is moving slowly to the east and slightly towards me. It gives the impression of an unstoppable advancing wave, bubbling up into billows.

I reposition myself for a different perspective. From the path, it looks as if a massive icy mountain range has risen behind the forest.

Is this cloud phenomenon an unusual event? Or has this been going on all of my life and I have just been unaware, too busy to stop and look up? I am amazed at how fast days fly by when I am out talking to trees and chasing clouds. It's growing late. It is late.

On a happier note, the Fundy bunnies are back. I had a great visit with tiny baby bun. She came right up to my feet on the stoop, as her mama browsed unconcerned in the nearby tall grass. Before retiring for the night, I stepped out on the back deck and almost crushed a mid-sized rabbit, maybe tiny baby bun's older brother.

As I lay down to sleep, the moon weaves in and out of long striated clouds. Even the sky is beginning to change, as autumn colors move in. Every night is just a bit cooler. Tonight I wear a fleece vest over my sweat suit. When I close my eyes, all that I can see are bunnies.

Day 34

Making do with a sufficiency in terms of space and material goods feels great. I can picture my son John visiting for the first time, standing in the middle of the room, looking around and saying, "I could live here." I know this about John because he, like me, is a minimalist.

Perhaps the most freeing innovation that I have added to my life over the past few years is downsizing. About ten years ago, I moved from a large condominium in a semi-urban, gated complex to a small cottage in a part of the Cape that is very quiet in the off-season.

I began to get rid of things. Initially a few here and there. I gained momentum. Just how many clothes does anyone need? I had far too many. First went the contents of one bureau, and then I freed up a closet for other uses. I felt lighter. Dishes, blankets, books (some of which I hadn't opened for twenty-five years), furniture that I would never use, odds and ends, bric-a-brac – all sold at yard sales or bundled up and delivered to the swap shop. I began to understand how much of an encumbrance all of this stuff had been, and decided to make it a rule to dispose of anything that I thought I might not use within the next year. Wow! Space really opened up!

Now I am at the point where virtually everything in my home either has some sort of immediate purpose or sentimental value, or is another living presence in the house, like the Christmas cactus that John gave me thirty-two years ago. I still have far too much, and I haven't missed a thing.

Patty and Bill are coming to dinner tonight. My table is set and my humble abode is made ready. I am preparing pasta and chicken with peppers and onions. It will be nice to have them here. They have been so good to me.

As I sit on the porch with my lunch, a light breeze passes over me. I notice the play of air and light, and the shadow on the ledge of the leaves of small birch trees. Like the late afternoon sun on the pond, this scene is a living, moving mosaic.

It seems that the longer I am here, the more definitively I exit myself and the more deeply I enter into a new dimension. I am growing liberated from an overbearing sense of pressure and, in its place, I am being filled with an almost childlike sense of awe and wonder.

For a moment I become fearful, and I can actually feel the presence of this fear in a palpable sense of contraction, a label that I have learned in my *dharma* reading. I am afraid that all of the gains will be lost when I return home, subsumed into the whirlwind of activity that awaits me.

I do have a choice. I can quit work, live on a greatly reduced income, and free up lots of time. But I would like to have more of a financial cushion for myself in my declining years. It doesn't feel like it is time yet to close up shop.

But then I am reminded that the birthing and support of this emerging sensitivity and awareness is not necessarily based upon my presence at the Dipper. Neither is it the extended time off, although this surely helps. The foundation is a consistent meditation practice. And that can travel wherever I go and can fit into a busy schedule. It is up to me to make it happen.

~

What a wonderful evening I had with my Canadian friends. They are a prolific source of information about the history and culture of New Brunswick and especially this area, as well as all kinds of helpful hints on living in the woods and near the sea.

Day 35

Up early, I leave on a long walk on this magical Sunday morning. The temperature is moderate, the air is moist, and the sun casts beams that glimmer on the leaves and bushes. Color is waning in the brush and long-gone in the grasses, but the green of the firs carries through all four seasons. Green. Blue. Brown. The constant colors of nature. How beautiful a tapestry they would make.

I saunter along, taking it all in – the birches, the alders with their dense berries, the raspberry bushes laden with fruit. The combined fragrance is indescribable. Rich and pungent. Woody and sweet. The essence of life bursting forth in fullness. Here only for a moment – only for a day.

~

Returning to the Dipper, it is time to make ready to go exploring the New Brunswick countryside. My UU friends, who do not meet for regular services in the summer, are having a picnic at Caroline and Tony's place, a country home in Upperton, about as far north of Saint John as I am to the south, and I am invited.

Passing by the airport, I made a little side trip to St. Martins, a scenic coastal fishing village with an old covered bridge. St. Martins is located at the southern end of Fundy National Park.

I found the countryside to be everything that I had anticipated and more. The fields, houses, and barns took me back in time to my childhood, as does so much of this Province. I remember going with my father to farms such as these in order to collect delinquent bills in the form of fresh vegetables.

Caroline and Tony's home is a pristine old farmhouse, which Tony, a skilled carpenter, has refinished over the years. It sits on over one hundred acres, with frontage of one-quarter mile on a major river. The farmer who owns the adjacent property grazes his cows and mows the hay in Caroline and Tony's fields. Places like this and the way of life that they afford, once prevalent in southern New England, have been all but lost.

Tony and Caroline set up a picnic spot on the riverside with the makings of a bonfire for roasting hot dogs and toasting marshmallows. Folks brought side dishes, folding chairs, and mosquito spray. I asked Tony if he had mosquitoes, and he jokingly responded, "How many would you like?" There was a great turn out for a Sunday afternoon toward the end of the summer.

The UU community is a mixture of people, many of who originally came from places other than Canada. There are folks from the Netherlands, Germany, Norway, and Great Britain, some of whom arrived here via a stay in the States. Several of my Quaker friends also originally came from the U.S.

Caroline and Doug put together a vesper service, including some campfire music, and Joost did a humorous reading. Once again, I was grateful to be part of this young and growing community as they celebrated life. No one seemed to mind a couple of party crashing cows from the adjoining pasture.

Day 36

With all this uninterrupted and consistent time for practice, meditation is really deepening. It is smooth this morning, like a lyrical melody. Thoughts intrude – usually some kind of planning. They slide off easily into the breath. In . . . out . . . .

I feel change coming on. The leaves of some of the birches and the small bushes are beginning to turn. Drained of their life substance, they burst forth in brilliant color.

On this Canadian early-autumn day, I pull my sleeves down

over my hands as I begin my walk. The crisp coolness of the air and the clean, fresh scent make each inhalation utter delight. I walk with gratitude for the opening of my senses and the emerging capacity to live in harmony with life as it is.

Walking through the woods, I reflect upon the pointed firs. In every stage of life and death, their roots and needles are constantly in transformation. Acceptance is their secret. Acceptance and surrender. Surrender into the wind. Surrender into each new day. Fearless, sink into the earth. From roots to shoots – let go.

Like the pointed firs, we rise and fall to re-enter life in different form. There are many divergent theories about an afterlife. Who knows, really? All I can contribute is a very simple belief – nothing is lost. Nothing.

Heading towards home, I encounter two women on horseback. Juanita, the owner of the two horses, tells me that she takes people on rides on the trails of the area. I think of daughter Annie and the "found" pony that she brought home. Annie and the pony were a great match until we discovered why the pony was lost and why no one claimed it. Cocoa was an escape artist, opening latches with his teeth and pushing down fence posts with his rump. I think that we finally foiled him with an electric fence. How Annie would love to ride these long and unspoiled New Brunswick paths with Juanita.

The butterfly encounters continue. Almost daily, particularly in sunny weather, an orange butterfly will present itself early on in my walk, leading me for a distance, and then disappearing.

What a special evening. I set my chair by the stoop in hopes that the bunnies would appear and approach me. And they did! First, a mid-size juvenile emerged from under the house and nibbled her way through the grass to my feet. She then sat up on her haunches, and within a few seconds her brother scampered onto the scene from somewhere behind me. These little guys have doubled their size since I first met them five weeks ago. They have to grow up fast in order to be ready for the Canadian winter.

Day 37

I walk in fleece today with my hood up. I briefly stop by a huge fir tree, its limbs draped with tattered strands of hanging lichen. I stretch out my arms to greet its outstretched branches. I move on, drawing my hands up into my sleeves against the cold. A light and joyful feeling arises. Like the nip in the air and the bunny on the stoop, joy takes me by surprise.

The wild raspberries are ready! They grow abundantly by the wayside, and they are now fully ripe. I eat them one at a time, and savor the experience of the many facets that together compose a raspberry.

Taking myself out for breakfast, I go to the little restaurant in the village that I refer to as Ruby's Place. I do not do this often, so it is a real treat. I order home-cooked oatmeal and decaf, and sit in the sunlight by the window – once again, as with the raspberries, savoring the experience.

On the way back, I revisit the tiny cottage on the cove. I walk the long pathway and climb the steps. Solidly constructed, it is tight against the weather. Roots of a family were laid down here. As I look out over the rocks to the sea, I imagine the sounds of small feet on the steps and children's voices in the air.

Back at the Dipper, I lay down for mid-day meditation. Much of the time, meditation is a struggle with my racing mind. However, as I am faithful to the practice, the breath is becoming an anchor, even outside of formal practice.

Late in the day, I lay on a ledge with my face toward the sun, covered by a baseball cap. Through an opening on the side I can see my backlit hair, brilliant in the sunshine. It is turning the most beautiful shade of silver – like my father's hair in his last years. Sometimes when I look in the mirror, I see his face, particularly his eyes.

Memories . . . Memories . . . Today I am transported back into the kitchen in my childhood home, coming in from play on a hot summer day. My mother lovingly handed me fresh-shelled peas in a little tin cup and fresh-squeezed lemonade in an ice-filled glass. I remember the same kitchen, a big electric mixer, and the makings of chocolate cake and extra-rich butter frosting. I would stand patiently waiting for bowls and spoons to lick. As I think about it, the tastes rise in my mouth.

I can never be in a railroad station, hear the sounds and be caught up in the flurry of activity, without remembering all the trips to the city on the train with Mom during the War, and the many soldiers and sailors coming and going . . . to home . . . to battle. This morning I awoke with a clear picture of my little blue-and-white, polka-dotted, freckle-faced rag doll, Becky.

Day 38

I headed into Saint John on this beautiful day. I swung by the waterfront, where there is a yearly festival. It begins this week and runs for several days. I then walked up to the Fire Museum, an old firehouse complete with antique apparatus. On the second floor there is a room of pictures of the great fire and its aftermath. I can't believe that folks who lived through the devastation ever recovered.

I passed the Imperial Theater, a beautiful old structure that has been entirely refurbished and now is used for all kinds of theatrical productions, including events staged by the local schools. At City Market, I treated myself to spinach salad, and then went for my customary swim at the Aquatic Center. Along the way I passed a talented young female violinist, who had set up shop in the passageway between City Market and the indoor mall. The walls are tile and the acoustics are magnificent.

On the way home, I stopped to purchase some much-needed hooded outer garments at the Salvation Army Store, and then made my customary swing up to the Pumpkin Patch for sugar-free vanilla ice cream. Returning to the Dipper, I stopped at the payphone to check in with Paul, Mom, and some of the children. As I pulled up the pathway, the fog was rolling in.

Day 39

Awakening early in the morning, I check my watch. It is 3:30 A.M. I look out over the meadow into a sky full of stars. A constellation hangs over the ledge.

Something has broken open, and the shell of my old life has fallen away.

The night air is cool. I inhale deeply of its clean, moist fragrance. The constellation fades out as the planet spins into a new day.

I call Mom about three times a week. She is always glad to hear from me, and pleased to know that I am happy. Today she asked, "Aren't you lonely yet?" I wonder if anyone really comprehends why I come here. I myself am just beginning to understand.

As an only child, I became used to playing alone and amusing myself. For me, the tiny wooded area behind my childhood home was magic. There was a little dirt road, an old shack, and a small field. I built tree forts and played in rock piles. I was a cowboy. I was strong and brave. Other little girls played with dolls. I performed surgery on mine.

I remember the long summer days lazing in the tall grass and watching clouds pass overhead. I remember the yellow wildflower that I would pull from the stem in order to suck the honey from the blossom, the coffee-ground weeds that I put into jars with punctured caps as beds for grasshoppers. I was almost always alone.

Those were formative years, and I was intoxicated. I would never recover. Although an entire adult life has intervened, in my core I am still that same child. My childhood shaped me and has called me back. Back to the small community and simpler life that I remember. Back to a more quiet and less cluttered environment. Back to the sounds, the smells, the bugs, the woods. Back to the freedom of a solitary little girl in her play-clothes in a very different time.

~

Late in the afternoon, I take a brief walk. A few wild roses cling to life, but, for the most part, the transition to autumn has begun. A yellow leaf appears on the deck as I write this. Several are floating on the pond. I came here in summer and will leave in the fall.

Day 40

This morning, the bats fascinate me. I mark their time. One passes every four seconds. Soaring, diving, careening toward the screen – one flies straight at me, reversing course in mid-flight. And then, suddenly and abruptly, they all disappear. Have they been here all through the night just below my level of vision? Is there an appointed moment for them to begin? To end?

As I start my walk today, mist is on my face. Drops of moisture hang from the tip of every branch. Fine, lacey grasses are laid flat by the dew. Tiny spider webs drape the outstretched limbs of the pointed firs. The air is rich with scents, each roaring forth its presence in the fog. Sunny days are plain – nice for arranged activities – but fog creates a feast for the senses.

A porcupine announces its presence with its distinctive squeaky-door sound. The greeting slides into a growl. I see him in the topmost branches of a birch tree, swinging back and forth in what would seem to be a precarious perch. We silently regard each other. I move on.

The color of the day is green, but with the hint of green passing. Orange, red, and yellow are beginning to show. Most grasses have gone brown. New Brunswick has reached the bottom of summer.

As I stand by the marsh, today's turn-around point on my walk, I notice that the flowers on the sweet-pea bushes have evolved into little pods. When did this happen? As I head toward home, fog has congealed into low, rapidly moving clouds. Everything seems to be on fast forward.

Almost every day since I came here, I have walked close to three miles. Three miles on a day when I have nothing else to do does not seem to be a lot. Figuring forty days so far, that makes one hundred twenty miles, almost the distance from here to the border and back again. It is amazing how much ground can be covered by going on one walk at a time.

Back at the Dipper, as I exercised while listening to the radio, my observations were validated by the comments of a man who wrote an article on his skirmish with a red squirrel. The public response to this piece was overwhelming. The red squirrels of New Brunswick are described as belligerent, intelligent, and skillful – burrowing their way into structures, and leaving a path of destruction in their wake. Folks are (jokingly) advised to arm themselves against these vicious little creatures. By the bye, one of the Dipper Harbour Gang is chattering at me from up on the ledge as I write this.

On a late-day walk to the beach, I find that the pathway has gone over to wildflowers in profuse bloom, some as high as my shoulder. A flock of small migratory birds lands along the tide line, foraging for food. They have such a long journey ahead. The tide changes, also heading out. I actually watch it happen. Such a miracle – twice every day.

Pausing on the path, I regard the Dipper. I am filled with joy and wonder at the perfection of this little hideaway. As a decision-making tool, "proceed as the way opens" has demonstrated its merit.

Day 41

Today I took a new route. Crossing the main road, I headed into the woods. I came to a field of high, lavender wildflowers, awash in bees and large orange butterflies. I watched, fascinated by the industry of all that tiny life.

As I moved to leave, a butterfly rose from the blossoms and zigzagged toward me. Turning in mid-air over my head, it landed on a flower directly in my path, spreading its wings to reveal their full, magnificent breadth. A living Compassionate Friends symbol, here in the woods.

Karen, my wild life rehabilitator friend from back in the States, lost both of her children in separate tragic events. She has devoted her life to healing wounded animals. I have watched her tend a dying crow, feed a baby bird, nurture a young possum. It is a privilege to know her.

Karen tells me that wild creatures are curious, and that, if we do not frighten them away, they may approach us. I certainly have found this to be true with the bunnies in my yard. Might this also not be the explanation for all the butterflies? My head says yes, but the irrational, trusting part of me believes that there is something else going on.

As I pass down a logging road, three wood thrushes converse. I stop to listen. Each calls from a different corner of the surrounding forest.

Day 42

The day breaks – cool and overcast. The sounds and vibrations of the sea are strong and constant. I get up, brew coffee, and sit on the porch through dawn.

On my morning walk, I am enveloped in fog, but with the bright glow of imminent clearing. On this late August day, it is deserted here. I stop and stand quietly. The fog is a living presence, altering perspective as I watch. In a moment's time, the grove at the corner is gone – then visible – then gone again.

In absolute stillness, the forest breathes, and I am still that solitary little girl in the woods of my childhood. I have been journeying all of my life to get here.

At first I hear it – the snort that announces a presence. And then they bound and leap across the path in front of me, white tails raised like flags. Deer. As they reach the brush, they stop and turn to look back at me. Big ears erect. Big eyes.

Yes, I am what I seem. Better not forget that you need to run. The hunters will soon be back.

Tonight, I sit on the porch and watch from dusk to dark. As the sun disappears, the pond surface is broken by expanding circles and darts, each created by a tiny insect. It looks like a colorless fireworks finale against a steel-grey sky.

Sitting quietly, I feel the first stirring of night – a tiny current carrying the smell of Fundy. Time passes. The air settles back into stillness. Animal sounds arise far off. I can feel myself sinking into this holy happening. The natural world is a crazy quilt in which all the pieces fit perfectly – and I am embroidered on.

Such peace. Such rest.

Tonight, I remember from *Walden*: "I grew in those seasons, like corn in the night . . . ." [3]

Day 43

I awoke this morning with my curiosity peaked about the Island of Grand Manan, a fishing port of note off the coast. Up early, I dressed in layers and left for Blacks Harbour, the site of the Grand Manan ferry dock. It was a cool and foggy day. The boat embarked with few passengers.

About mid-way along, the sun broke through and folks alerted me to schools of dolphins off both port and starboard. I was told to keep my eyes open, as it is not unusual to see whales from the Grand Manan ferry.

The Island loomed ahead, a massive rampart, its rock sides rising vertically from the sea. A stark and angular lighthouse greeted us on a point of land adjacent to the ferry slip.

I explored the village and the extensive fishing facility, and then headed out to Swallowtail Light. Approachable only via a narrow footbridge, the trails on the lighthouse promontory are high and occasionally precarious. I made my way out to an oceanfront bench and lolled in the sun, watching seals swim in and out of the fish weirs at the bottom of the cliff. A return trip ferryboat came – and went – as I stayed on.

On the way back toward town, I made a side excursion to Hole-in-the-Wall Park, a campground with hiking trails and observation platforms. I inquired about camping, thinking of a possible visit next year with Linda, Alyssa, and Mark. The attendant told me of campsites perched on the very verge of cliffs rising hundreds of feet from the sea. She assured me that other options were available.

I purchased a roll of film and headed back to catch the next boat. Almost at the docks, I realized that I had left the film behind. On my way back to the campground to retrieve my purchase, I encountered the attendant heading into town to deliver my film to me.

As the boat rounded Swallowtail Light, I regarded the eagles' nest campsites, as I conversed with two people from the States who had spent a week at Hole-in-the-Wall. They described moonlit evenings looking out over the sea and watching whales and dolphins at play, and falling asleep at night to the sounds of the spouting breath of whales off shore.

Alone on the upper deck, I gazed out over the water. I thought of Emma and one of the many things that I learned from her brief visit. To live deep is to live in the knowledge of the ineffable nature of life. Daily we tread the narrow ridge of paradox. To have the view, we must risk the fall.

I arrived home as I had left – surrounded by fog.

Day 44

This morning, as last night's fog lifts, the dawn sky is grey, with huge white cirrus feathers lining the horizon.

What a one-of-a-kind summer this has been. I am witnessing the recovery of the land. Every inch supports life of some kind. The pond is awash with frogs, whirligigs, and dragonflies. The two ducks return almost daily, and the bunnies have taken up residence. The babies seem totally acclimated to my presence, but Mama still sits up tall and alert when I approach, moving her ears to and fro.

Everything is wet from the fog. Pages of my journal hang moist, and the cover of a book that I just purchased has curled. Bushes and grasses glisten in the morning light.

This morning, I headed out to the field of lavender flowers. Although the blossoms remained, there was not a butterfly in sight.

As I walked the main road, several work trucks bearing fishing gear and fishermen passed by. Without fail, a hand was raised from the steering wheel in greeting. Weathered hands. Hands hard from toil on the sea.

I know nothing about fishing. I can only imagine the life of a fisherman. Perhaps more than any other job, fishing really puts you *out* there. Dependent upon and subject to the elements, that boat is alone. I have seen how fast the Fundy weather conditions can change.

There must be something unique in the character of fishermen, formed by a life at sea and fed by the necessity of adaptation, ingenuity, and courage. I can imagine how the sea could get into the blood. I can understand how a fisherman could be rendered unfit for other jobs. How could a fisherman sit at a desk in a cubicle all day – or even drive a truck?

Evening falls. The slant of the sun casts a white glow upon the ledge. Slowly the light moves up and into the trees as the sun falls to the horizon, turning the crowns to gold. Golden crowns for this perfect day in the north woods.

I retire early, but am awakened by a tiny rattling sound. I rise to peek out. I had left an animal trap on the deck. It had sprung shut, but there was still a little peanut butter on the plate. I watch a mouse squeeze through a hole in the mesh about the size of the tip of my index finger.

Day 45

This morning, the air hangs in silence. No leaf stirs. Even the sea is still. Lying in my sleeping bag, I hear a noise like the sound of a fan. I look up to see a large flock of geese passing over in the form of a ragged *V*. North to south they fly, heralding the change of season. Soon they are followed by another group . . . and then another.

Preparing for the time ahead, I go into town to the market. Family is coming here soon. As I return from the pay phone and drive up the wooded path, a thunderstorm materializes out of nowhere. A bolt of lightning flashes from the sky. I respond instantly with an involuntary shudder and gasp. And then, after a few drops of rain, it is over. I am dumb with wonder.

Since I have been here, eating only healthy food, I have become well to the extent that I can detect changes in how I feel when I ingest salt, sugar, or fat. I am also noticing how much better I feel overall when I drink substantial quantities of water. I especially notice this when I take long and vigorous walks. My joints actually feel less stiff and more lubricated.

Later in the day, I stopped at the Coastal Enterprises office to say hello to Shirley. I then swung around to the village, pausing at the fork in the road to regard a small white building with a "Dipper Harbour" sign hung in between and just above the sole front window and the door. I wondered what the building might have been in the past. Solid, unpretentious, enduring – it is characteristic of these people and this place that I have come to love.

Day 46

This morning, I sit by the pond for a long time. The whirligigs seem to assemble in shallow spots against the shore, breaking out in mass confusion when I approach. As the sun rises, they begin to make excursions, trailing their cruising wakes. They are like tiny water-borne bumper cars careening headlong into one another.

I notice what appears to be a struggle toward the middle of the water. Apparently a dragonfly has skimmed a little too close to the surface, dipped a wing, and plunged into the pond. Whirligigs are attacking ferociously. Surely they are not going to eat this insect that is many times their size. I leave for a moment to get my field glasses for a closer look. When I return, there is no dragonfly in sight, and the whirligigs are re-engaged in their foraging activity.

A frog emerges from the water and sits on the shore, awaiting dinner. The pond is alive! There is aquatic plant life on the bottom, and a few cattails are springing up. It is just another community. I lose myself in the shimmering water and the midday warmth.

As I turn to leave, I notice something floating. I check it out with the binoculars. Two whirligigs have positioned themselves atop a piece of bark. Tiny oval life forms, each complete within itself, basking in the sun. A small orange snake slithers across the pond. Nimble and at home in its element, it dives out of sight.

Today is taken up with preparing for a joyfully anticipated family visit and packing up what I can for my return trip to the Cape. As I take a last solitary walk, a big orange butterfly leads me up the road, and, as I turn the corner back to the Dipper, two others alight in my path.

I am noticing that I feel different. Not just in some superficial way. It's more that I feel lighter, as if a burden is lifting.

This summer, I have been away for forty-five days. I was gone for thirty-one days in the spring. Folks got along without me. People ran their own lives. I don't have to take care of everything. I am loved for who I am. I can let go of the past and all of the 'if onlys.' I can let go of the future and the 'what ifs.'

Breathing out, it all falls away.

Day 47

Up early. It's time for the first family visit! I meet Kathy, Jim, Kendall, and Derrick at the border for the start of a whirlwind weekend.

After a stop at the Blueberry Patch for sundaes and at the market in St. George for a few groceries, we had lunch at the Dipper and spent the afternoon walking the environs. We then had a lovely dinner at Ruby's Place and made sleeping arrangements. Kendall will sleep on the porch with me. The rest of the family will stay at the nearby Mariner, a lovely New Brunswick inn perched on a hilltop overlooking the Bay of Fundy.

The next day was spent in Saint John, enjoying the city and especially the Aquatic Center, where Derrick and Jim particularly liked the high diving board. We then came back to the Dipper and went to the beach. Derrick gathered wood and Jim prepared a bonfire. No permit is needed here, as there is no one who would object. With neighbors in attendance, marshmallows were toasted as we watched the sun go down.

Days 48-51

Kathy, Jim, and Kendall left early in the morning, and Derrick stayed here with me. An outdoorsy kid, virtually everything about the place was enjoyable for him. We hiked the trail past Torie's land into the woods where I previously would not venture alone, reaching a pristine rocky beach. We christened this spot Echo Cove, as our voices echoed off the surrounding cliffs. We took long walks down the moose trails and out to the bog. Derrick thrived in the camp environment, even pitching in and doing chores.

We ended our time in New Brunswick with a visit to Patty and Bill's farm. Patty showed Derrick the animals, and Bill sent us off with his warm and wonderful prayer for travel graces.

So, here I am at the end of a second extended time away. The place is becoming familiar and comfortable to the degree that it feels like home. But it isn't home. Home is where I left my heart. Home is with my family.

Tonight the air is still – and I reflect upon how I have become an adventurous old woman . . . on fire with the love of life.

AUTUMN

Day 1

The ride up was great. I stopped at my favorite break place, Dysart's Truck Plaza, near Bangor, Maine. The ambience is wonderful. Acres of trucks of every size, shape, and description: trailer trucks, riggers, cattle trucks; trucks carrying logs, crushed stone, lumber; double trucks, trucks towing trucks. Husband and wife truckers in matching outfits. Truckers with dogs, big and small. A father trucker with his little boy who obviously adores his Dad and loves to sit at the truckers' table. Refrigerated trucks. Trash trucks. Trucks hauling hay, cars, oil. Women truckers, svelte and dapper truckers, and guys with their bellies hanging over their belt loops.

The facility includes a barbershop, showers, a laundromat, a recreation room, banks of telephones, a truck brokerage desk, a great highway store and souvenir shop, not to mention a wonderful restaurant with two dining rooms. There are truck grills built into the walls, and pictures of trucks carrying all kinds of loads, especially logs. The waitresses are pros, and they call you "Hon" or "Sweetie." The food is good and reasonably priced, and the servings are generous. I sat facing the window, enjoying the constant movement of vehicles, and honoring my son Craig and his profession.

I arrived at the Dipper somewhat late on a golden autumn day. After unpacking and setting up shop on the porch, I zipped myself into my sleeping bag with only my face exposed to the brisk, nippy movement of the evening air. I fell asleep almost as soon as my head hit the pillow.

The next thing that I knew, crows were calling. The sunrise was blue with low grey clouds, appearing as if painted on in broad childlike brush strokes. All of this is now blessedly familiar, as the Dipper begins to work its spell.

Day 2

Waiting for the sun to take my body with its warmth, I watch a beam of light slide down the cabin wall. A wave or particle? Or both? A stumbling block for science. Nothing but another mystery for me. I am witness to the turning of the world, as the hand with which I write now casts a shadow. A great unknowable and mysterious energy moves night into day.

I have no words to say how much I relish this quiet and peace. Simply lying in the early morning sun, I feel whole.

Beginning my morning walk, I am greeted by the fragrance of New Brunswick – light, salty, and sweet with the scent of Christmas. Prayer upwells in me in words not of my making.

I pass a thick, dark wood, fragrant with earth, dense with the decay of old growth. Small patches of light break through. Lichen hangs from dead inner fir branches. The place speaks of time and passage. Returning home, I find the Dipper almost aglow in this special autumn light.

A curious thing is happening to me. As I attend to the breath in meditation, natural events in the passing of the day are catching me off-guard with their immediacy. The light touch of the breeze gently lifting my shirt. The thought-stopping impact of smells. And tonight, the sight of common things – a bowl of fruit cast into focus by a certain quality of light. There is this something that seems to pass through it all, and what is new is that I am now aware of it in my direct experience.

Autumn nights are really cool. I have sewn together the sides of a woolen blanket, and I use it as an external pouch for my sleeping bag. Retiring early, I fall into the sleep of the gods.

Day 3

Today is a task day. Rise and shine.

The light reflected off the cliff casts an image on the gently moving surface of the autumn pond in a grey, brown, and green mosaic pattern. One last frog remains. He had better start digging down soon.

The day passes quickly. I take a run into St. George and pick up ingredients at the Whole Food Store. I return home and make a huge pot of soup. Now I feel really settled in.

As I zipper in on the porch, an animal sound arises from the ledge, beginning soft and muffled. Then a second voice joins in – clearly an owl. The two voices seem to be in dialogue. After a time they move off, making two stops and then disappearing.

Day 4

Today I am up and out for an early morning walk. Most of the foliage is gone, with the exception of alder leaves, which hang on, dry and brittle, click-clacking against one another in the breeze.

Prayer is on my mind this trip. I believe that the holy people down through time, like Jesus of the Christians, Mohammed of the Moslems, the prophets of the Jews, Buddha, Lao Tze, are fingers pointing at the source. Prayer, for me, arises from contact with that source.

Because I am a praying person, Zen does not entirely fit, so just what is it that I am doing? On my walk, my best pondering time, it occurred to me that the precepts of Zen and the example of Jesus provide a way to live, and that prayer and meditation are a way of life. Reading reinforces practice, and Quaker meeting supports prayer.

During my time back in Wellfleet the past few weeks, my precious meditation practice all but slipped away. When I returned to the States, I quickly became caught up in the business of every day and the constant push for closure. This habitual behavior could continue until I ultimately bundle up my life and cash it in. Only then will there be no next thing to do. In the meantime, that special quality of light in the autumn sky will have passed by while I was busy doing other things. Deep life does not wait for all the projects to be completed. My daily activities will roll over me if I don't do battle with the inertia.

When I return home, I will try to keep the practice by consciously honoring dawn, midday, and dusk – each with a bow and a five-minute silent presence. I can do this no matter what is going on. I will make a commitment to do what I know that I will do, and not attempt to do what I can do and won't. That's a start.

The day comes and goes. I meditate. I walk. I read. I end the day sitting by savoring a cup of decaf coffee. The view over the meadow to the grove is breathtaking in the autumn light. The low slant of the late day October sun casts the white birch trees in brilliant relief against the darkening sky.

Day 5

Last night, I watched a moonrise over the ledge. The moon slipped in and out from behind huge clouds. The stones on the porch were luminescent in the moonlight.

Awakening into meditation, I am caressed by the clean morning air and serenaded by the foghorn. Snug in my sleeping bag, I meditate on and on. I feel the coolness of the air as I draw it in through my nostrils. I have no desire to get up. Being is the only doing.

I sip my coffee in the creaking cabin, as I watch the weather begin to change.

I walk slow and easy this morning. I pause at a spot overlooking the sea, and listen to the muffled sloshing of the Fundy tide, quiet as the whisper of air that moves the branches. No one is here. Peace settles over my body.

Today the sea is the color of cold and hard steel. Steel-grey sea – as hard as the men who work it, and as cold as they soon will be out there on the winter water.

I continue on to the marsh. Fall color in New Brunswick is a combination of muted shades of yellow and rust and the four seasons green of fir. I think that there is nothing so spectacular as the October landscape, cast into brilliant perspective by the low slant of the sun against the darkening sky. Colors are almost aglow in the waning autumn light. A last burst of glory in the face of the onslaught of winter.

Heading back to the Dipper, I bushwhack through some brush and crest a rock ledge. I am caught up short by the experience of red. Low berry bushes are backlit by the early morning sun. Crimson? Scarlet? No. Deeper and more vibrant. I pick a leaf and examine it. Without the penetration of the sun and the juxtaposition of other leaves, it is pretty, but ordinary. It is the community of blazing life that takes my breath away.

In a spirit of play and celebration, I clear around a tiny fir tree and christen it with a faded red neckerchief, a garland, and an ornament. I will watch it grow and share special occasions with it.

Today I am searching for a name with which to address this life force that is becoming increasingly manifest to me. In my private discourse there is no difficulty. All manner of word-forms spill from me, but, back in the States, I am planning a more regular attendance at Quaker meetings. God is spoken of there. What is my resistance to that naming?

A product of teachings steeped in doctrine, the God of my youth is divisive and exclusive, judgmental and punitive – an all-or-nothing creation of the religious elite. This is a God that has gotten into politics and denies condoms to the AIDS-ravaged poor of Africa.

I try on "Tao," the Eastern identification of True Emptiness, and "Wakan Tanka," the Sioux term for Great Mystery. Both are God concepts that I find agreeable, but not appropriate for public usage in Western culture. I would have to explain and re-explain.

So – how am I to speak of it? Of no substance, yet present in all substance, this purveyor of bunnies and butterflies. I put the question to the pointed firs.

~

Well, it's Saturday night and time for an old-fashioned, country community roast beef dinner, put on by the all-volunteer Musquash Fire Department. The fire persons (there are women) and the Auxiliary prepare and serve a full-course meal to a packed house. I very much enjoyed the food and camaraderie, and especially the company of a retired woman who sat across from me at the end of a long table. When it was time to go, she invited me to visit for coffee, and even gave me directions to her home.

On the porch, I slip into my sleeping bag on the darkest night ever. Absolutely no visibility at all.

Day 6

Thick fog rolls in as I arise. The fragrances of the New Brunswick coast hang in the air. I love the dampness – the tiny drippings of a foggy day. When I was on a long trip to the western U.S., where there is virtually no humidity, my lips became dry and my skin felt taut. Here on the Fundy coast, I feel green, alive, watered.

It is 8 A.M. The sun is breaking through. In a flash – like a regiment of soldiers standing erect and ready – the pointed firs emerge from the fog, and then, just as quickly, disappear again.

I lay on my back with my hands on my stomach. I feel a strong pulse as blood courses through me. My breath rises and falls. I contemplate the miracle of human life. I recently read that meditation, for some Native People, is sitting and listening to the heartbeat.

It's Sunday, and I'm off to St. Andrews for Quaker Meeting. It is amazing how fast sixty minutes of sitting can fly by. Quaker silence is not silence as a respite from sound. Neither is it reflective silence, or the silence of a pause with something to follow. It combines these things, but it is much more. Quaker silence gathers energy unto itself. Quaker silence is living presence – each of us to the other, and all of us to the Light. It is lush. It is exquisite. And it is also nothing at all.

Before going our separate ways, my friends and I gathered for informal talk over blueberry pie and tea. These bright, unpretentious, and compassionate folks have become the northern extension of my tribe.

Back at the Dipper, off in the distant falling night, I see two lights – one pale blue, the other amber. As flecks moving across the sea toward the horizon, they disappear into the darkness.

Day 7

Early in the morning I awake to a moonset. To the west a cloud cover has moved in. The moon lights the sky behind it, creating the play of dark and light in shades of grey and silver. The clouds resemble long, torn, contrasting strands of ragged fabric. The entire mass changes moment by moment. On the opposite horizon, the first light of dawn appears.

The clouds roll back to reveal the naked moon, full and as bright as I have ever seen. Then they begin to break up, trailing behind wisps and filaments. The moon settles amongst the spires of the pointed firs. They receive her motionlessly. Nothing stirs, and then she is gone, leaving a grove of ghostly, backlit trees.

I look down to write. I look up. The clouds have blended with the early morning sky as if nothing has ever happened. The pointed firs have fallen back into line. It's over, and I am once again reminded of how very small I am in the big picture.

Setting the ticker for thirty minutes, I settle down to meditate. When I arise it will be day, and for most of the people in the world, nothing will have happened.

The spell is broken by the song of a bird. White clouds turn into cirrus streaks far overhead on another cool morning here in the True North. Inside the cabin, a film of moisture has formed on the windows, as I add a down vest and a second pair of woolen socks. My breath condenses into a visible mist.

Later, at the beach, the tide is low and the air has warmed. I browse. I sit. Turning toward home, I notice a line of timbers well up onto shore, some actually catapulted into the woods by a stormy sea. Huge tree trunks, beams of ships, telephone poles, tangles of detritus – parts of which are as wide as a man – all at least twenty vertical feet above the tide line and fifty feet inland from the same point. A reminder of the fury of Fundy. The small storms that I have witnessed are awesome enough. I can't imagine the power of the wind and wave that created this massive wash-up.

Tonight the moon has the appearance of an opaque eye. It seems like forever since I first faced my fear and slept on the porch. Settling into my sleeping bag to dissolve into the night has become the highlight of my time here.

 I read myself to sleep. More Zen. As I drift off, a faint breeze, light as a breath, wafts through the screens and gently moves my hair. And then – from out of nowhere . . . *Yahweh* . . .

 Yes, maybe . . .

Day 8

 It is a grey autumn day, threatening rain. Stark. Base. Elemental. The North Country at its bleakest best.

 Lena, the little girl from Belarus who visited with Betty and Lars last summer, came to mind this morning. She has gone home, but there is no question that she has been changed by her stay in this place and with these people. We all are changed when we step out of our insularity and connect with the larger world. Lena's future will be different because, even at such a young age, her vision has been widened.

 The huge cloud cover rolls out, replaced by blue sky and low, fast moving cumulus. Sitting on the stoop, I am warmed by the sun. It feels healthy and life-giving. I can see why snakes and turtles like to bask. I peruse the yard on this brisk, cool morning. Nature's art is everywhere.

 My attention is drawn to loud, raspy squawks, as three blue herons fly overhead. Two move off toward the sea, and one flies in a different direction – alone.

~

 As I sit in my lounge chair looking out over the meadow, I think about the career that chose me. Back when I returned to school, I was a single mother. Only one college offered a degree program that fit into my life. Three majors were available: History, English, and Psychology. I had a large family. I chose the major that afforded the best opportunity for a paying job as soon as possible.

 I am not sorry that I became a Psychologist. I consider it a great privilege to be invited into the lives of others, and I am good at what I do, probably because I like people, and also because I myself have had a difficult life. My woundedness underlies my effectiveness.

Most people who come to see me have suffered some kind of a loss. Loss of a loved one. Loss of health. Loss of trust – of hope. Loss of self-respect. Most people seek healing. All healing requires time, and most healing implies change. I am not the healer. Time and a healing environment are the keys.

I came to the Dipper after Emma's death following an intuition. I have walked the quiet paths as I let New Brunswick have its way with me. So – what am I finding, tucked into the woods by the Bay of Fundy? I am finding the keys. Healing rises up through the roots here. Change rides the tides.

As evening falls, I try on Yahweh. Recognizable in Western culture, but free of hooks. Soft and light, it rolls off the tongue. Suitable to invoke in passion or to whisper in gratitude or adoration.

Yahweh . . .

Day 9

Early this morning a cloud cover hangs heavy. The trees on the ledge seem drawn on as if by charcoal. I glance over my shoulder. The first brightness of dawn breaks in a pocket on the horizon. It is like looking into a reverse cave – a cave of light. It seems as if thousands of beings of all kinds are poised – watching, waiting.

I am lying in the confluence of forest and sea, and nothing speaks or moves. Life is suspended, as the maw of the cave of light enlarges. A bird sings a few tentative notes, and then stops. A spear of light moves over the ledge. The stillness is broken by the slightest movement of air over the back of my neck.

I can now see across the pond and into the woods. Lines of muted color emerge. Large birds alight in the water. Shorebirds? Ducks? It is still too dark to tell. They browse amongst the new reeds, gently stirring the pond surface. Sensitive to my presence, they fly away at the slightest evidence of movement. And – in an instant – something has shifted. Day! It is now day!

Lying on my stomach to meditate, I take long, deep breaths. My entire body rises and falls. And then, once again, monkey mind is at work. Thoughts race every which way. I remember the *dharma*. I observe the thinker and feel the contraction engendered by the thoughts. I observe. I feel. Thoughts and emotions fade. I count breaths ... in ... out ...

Later, in the city for my usual routine, I stopped at the library to check the history and usage of "Yahweh." Apparently it has something to do with the verb "to be," and is especially related to that phrase from Scripture, "I am that I am." No past or future. Unchanging. Uncomplicated. So far, so good. I stopped at a religious bookstore. No books about Yahweh and no reference to Yahweh in doctrinal treatises. It's clean. It's not loaded.

"I am that I am." There is nothing more to be said.

I go for a late-day walk through the woods. Sometimes the scenes I come across literally take my breath away. Rock ledges are draped with a mantle of rust-orange, as the low berry bushes give up the ghost for another year.

Night falls quietly. As I assume my meditation posture in my sleeping bag, the air changes to the cool sharpness and definition of evening. It will be dark. It will be dark – and enchanted.

Day 10

Wide awake at 4 A.M., I struggle to find words to convey the feeling of night here. The surf is up. An occasional wave rips into the shore or thuds against the rocks. The wind rustles the screens. I am so small against this vast design. I recall a line from Scripture: " ... And who am I that You should take notice of me . . . ?"

I am perplexed. After weeks of terrible suffering, our beautiful little baby girl died. I buried You with my granddaughter when her tiny white coffin was lowered into the ground. But You have refused to go. And now – I can give You a new name, but I cannot give You up.

~

As I arise at 7 A.M., a big storm is on the way, with large amounts of rain predicted. The surf sounds a constant roar, with the occasional thud of a big breaker. The wind whistles through the screen and blows cool on my face. Daybreak is but a transition from muted charcoal to a lighter grey. There will be no sun for a long while. I hope that the fishing boats are all in. High winds have been predicted, along with flooding of the Saint John River.

I take a ride into the village of Dipper Harbour on this dark autumn day. The place is deserted, and the docks and their reflection are cast in a ghostly air. The fishermen will soon be switching over to lobstering.

I stop at the pay phone to check in with Paul. There have been no emergencies. All is quiet.

Paul and I shared office space for several years. Like me, Paul has no brothers or sisters. Two only children, we adopted each other as siblings. It has been an interesting arrangement. I tested the relationship on an occasion when I dislocated my shoulder. In the midst of a New England blizzard, I was taken to the hospital by ambulance. I called Paul for a ride home. "Are you really my brother?" I asked. "Yes, tomorrow when the snow stops," he replied.

Tonight, I am thinking about Mom's recent ninetieth birthday party. It was a wonderful family event. We all had a chance to tell something special about Grandma. I was surprised at some of the memories of little things from way back that were shared by family members. She has surely been an important person in everybody's life and a constantly available source of nurturance.

I slept in, with the rain pelting the Dipper in waves and bursts. Even inside the cabin I could hear the brook pouring down into the pond. This is real weather.

Day 11

Awakening early, I could not sleep. I am accustomed to spending my nights on the porch. The cabin felt close, in spite of the fact that I had the windows open.

The rain has been steady and heavy, and the wind is constant. A small tree has fallen over in the meadow. It is October in New Brunswick, and the storms have begun.

This morning, I am awash in the sound of water. The sea pounds into the rocks. Inside the house, it feels as if heavy machinery is being worked nearby. Water runs from the roof in torrents. The pond reels in bursts of wind and rain-driven patternless designs. The brook rushes down in a mini-waterfall. Such a wonderful adventure it is to be here.

What a treat! Caroline and Tony came to the Dipper for early dinner. We took our time, spending the afternoon in a long and stimulating kitchen-table chat over crackers and cheese, home made soup, and tea. I really love their company. Like so many of the Canadians that I have met, they have a broad and intelligent understanding of and respect for life beyond the borders of their own country. We talked of tipping points – both political and environmental, and balances that cannot continue to be disregarded.

Pondering into the night, I thought of the global village that is emerging – rapidly now in this war-weary world. I believe that insular societies will implode, as events force the recognition and acceptance of people from the Third World as our neighbors.

Folks I know who have spent extended time in China tell me that new cities are springing up seemingly overnight. Outsourcing is becoming a common business practice. Professionals from Third World countries are gaining expertise. Even medicine is now internationally linked. The MRI that I got at a hospital on Cape Cod may have been read by a specialist in India. The Third World is entering the twenty-first century as a cog in the turning economic wheel, and not just a source of cheap labor.

Whatever will all this become? Perhaps something better, if we can endure the changes with hope and patience.

Day 12

Folks have been telling me about Fredericton, the Capitol of the Province, and the popular Saturday morning farmers' market. "Go early," they all say, "because the crowds get really heavy after 10 A.M."

Route 7, the most direct connection between here and Fredericton, is lined with huge moose alert signs, some with flashing lights. Some people who commute between Saint John and the Capitol have told me that they will not travel that road at night. I took everyone's advice, left early, and arrived at 8:30 A.M.

Housed in two buildings, the Boyce Farmers' Market exceeded all of my expectations. There were booths of all kinds, selling such things as organic vegetables, meat and fish, farm-fresh eggs, jewelry, crafts, leather goods, clothing, pastry, especially the highly recommended "bee sting," a scrumptious crème-filled square. Out in the yard there was more: fresh-cut flowers, additional crafts booths, fruits and vegetables, and a food court with all kinds of ethnic dishes.

The most popular spot was the samosa stand, which offered a choice of meat or vegetable in mild or hot. The line wound well out into an aisle. I bought a mild turkey at the price of seventy-five cents, and went back for two more.

I then struck out on a self-guided walking tour. The city sits on the bank of the Saint John River, which is still wide at this point. Buildings are old and charming, and include a barracks and guard house that goes back to the British presence in the early 1800's. A changing-of-the-guard procession occurs daily. A small contingent of red-coated soldiers with pipes and drums march through town in order to keep the tradition established by the First Royal Regiment.

The Legislative Assembly Building was constructed in the late 1880's, and is still used for meetings of Parliament. All the old wood is polished to a sheen. The place still retains its original charm.

I walked toward the river, passing art galleries and an exquisite old Anglican Cathedral. I crossed a railroad trestle that has been converted to a footbridge. The views from midway across the river back toward town to the hillside campuses of the University of New Brunswick and Saint Thomas University are beautiful.

The city can boast of wide neighborhood sidewalks, tree-lined streets, and lovely old houses. Like the people of Saint John, the folks of Fredericton are welcoming and enthusiastic about their hometown.

I took myself out for a lovely salad at the James Joyce Pub, a groggery with eats, similar to the pubs that Linda and I visited when we toured the countryside of England and Wales. What a great day of exploration this turned out to be.

~

I arrived back at the Dipper at dusk, and spent the evening playing my Native American flute. It is hard to describe how deeply the pathos of the Native People touches me. It is almost as if I have lived through the horror of the past with them.

I first felt this on my trip west with Dane, when we stayed on the Sioux Reservation in South Dakota. From the little casement window in my room at the Wakpamni Bed and Breakfast, I looked out over the vast night fieldscape and felt the presence of familiar spirits from long ago. When Caroline and Tony were here, we talked about the possibility of having had other lives. Caroline says that she identifies with black culture in such a way that she feels as if she has personally lived it.

Day 13

I decided to go into town on this Sunday morning to join the Unitarians. As I walked in the door, Wendy, the pianist, was playing an obscure slow and melodic song that was on one of Emma's musical tapes. It would be playing frequently when I visited her in the hospital. Just yesterday I played the very same melody on my flute. What are the chances that Wendy would have selected this song for today?

This was ministerial Sunday. Kitsy, a UU minister from Portland, Maine, comes on an extended visit once a month to conduct a Sunday service and make herself available to the congregation in any way that they might need her. The service was beautiful, as usual. On Kitsy's Sundays in town, parishioners have lunch with her. I joined them at a local Tim Hortons.

Later in the afternoon, I attended a writing group, "Dropped Threads," with Kitsy and Martha, the Director of Music for the UUs. We chatted for a while, and then got to writing, using the sentence stem, "Back in that time . .", as a jump-off. Kitsy and I agreed that we will be among the last people who will actually remember the

U.S. of World War II and rationing stamps first hand.

During the war, meat and sugar were a luxury. I can still see Dad reaching into his pocket for the green, gas ration stamp book. No new cars were manufactured, and tires were virtually unavailable. Folks drove to and from work, and that was it. Shoes were resoled, and one new pair per year was the norm. Silk for stockings was used in parachutes. Much of the country's resources went into the feeding and clothing of the armed forces. Everyone participated in the war effort in some way. My three young uncles were in the Navy in the Pacific. My father worked in the shipyard. This was a U.S. of modest means – of simple lives. This was a U.S. that did without and pulled together for a greater good. If our earth is to be healed, this may need to happen again.

Back home, as night set in, the rain began. It was dark and gloomy in a way that only places near the sea can be. As I pulled into my yard and got out of the car, a single blue heron circled directly overhead two times – and then flew away.

Day 14

Last night I slept on the porch in the rain. Sleep-inducing water sounds kept me down until 9:00 this morning.

I am studying *The National Audubon Society Field Guide to Weather*. I have owned this book for years and this is the first time that I have read it at any depth. Today is a cloudwatcher's cornucopia. Fast moving scud. Streaky grey stratocumulus. High cumulus with cirrus streamers – some with filigreed edges. Canada Geese streak across the sky headed south, where I will be going shortly.

This morning I am looking forward to reconnecting with my friends at the Mass. Audubon Wellfleet Bay Wildlife Sanctuary, where I spend a good portion of my time back in the States. Like Irving Nature Park, Wellfleet Bay is composed of several ecosystems. I walk trails through forest, heathland, and saltmarsh, by ponds, and along a sandy beach. There are deer, otter, heron, and seals. Come to think of it, the wildlife population is similar to that of New Brunswick except that there are more skunks and fewer porcupines, more hawks and fewer eagles. I consider it a privilege to be part of the

Audubon organization, which serves to preserve the environment and to educate future generations about the marvels of nature.

Wellfleet Bay is currently engaged in a building campaign. The new buildings will be amongst the greenest structures in the U.S. Along with my family, the Audubon Sanctuary is my strongest anchor in the States. Barbara, a fellow Naturalist, says that church for her is Silver Spring Trail on a Sunday morning. Amen, I say to that!

Standing on my stoop, my back against the screen door, I look up. A cloud in the shape of a butterfly drifts overhead. And then a solitary Great Blue Heron swoops down over the pond and lands on a log, perhaps thirty feet from me. I become still as a statue. He seems to regard me curiously for a few moments. Then he turns and paces the log its length, surveying the pond. He stops and proceeds to groom himself. In my past life, I would have been carrying a camera, and, in attempting to take a picture, I would have driven him away.

He then assumes a position of rapt attention. Head and neck extended outward, he slowly lifts one leg and then the other. He advances forward in movements that visually define stealth. And then, with a rapid thrust, he takes a frog. Something draws his attention. He extends his neck up like a periscope, almost doubling his size. The wind ripples the feathers on his chest. He is magnificent.

I move. He leaves, raising massive wings and lifting off on a current of wind with effortless grace. I look up. The butterfly is gone.

Day 15

This morning, I awake to a changing sky. A dark grey cloud cover lies over the Bay of Fundy in a poker-straight line, in vivid contrast with the white sky lower on the horizon. A tiny blue patch materializes – and then another – and another. How quickly this happens. I look down, and look back up again. The blue is gone. And then I hear it – the day's first wash of ocean water!

As I leave on my walk, the pointed firs sway to and fro, waving their branches in frenetic movement. The air is charged with energy. A fine mist begins to materialize. The wind becomes stronger, and the mist feels like pin pricks on my face. I have become a tissue of senses. I breathe with the forest. My heart beats with the sea.

I go to the water and look out to the south. The tide is coming in quickly. I stand on a cliff for a long time. The foghorn sounds. I climb down to the beach, sit on a rock, and let the tide wash in around me. Yahweh rolls in on the billows.

Returning to the Dipper, I hear the occasional report of a rifle. The hunters are here. Time to dig out the orange vest.

Ending the day with an indoor walking meditation, I set up a candle on top of an inverted urn and light some incense. Shutting off the lights, I walk ever so slowly in small circles around the room, focusing on each footfall. Shifting pressure – heel to toe, side to side – as evening moves in on sheets of rain.

I sleep in, with the wind-driven rain pelting the Dipper in waves and bursts. Even inside the cabin, I can hear the brook pouring down into the pond.

Day 16

Awakening in the middle of the night, I couldn't get back to sleep. As I lay there, attempting meditation, my thoughts kept returning to the radio and the Canadian National Anthem, with which the station begins the programming day. Eventually I got up, went inside, and did a few tasks. Having forgotten about the anthem and neither knowing or caring what time it was, I turned on the radio to hear the last few words of a broadcast from Prague, followed immediately by the strains of "O Canada." Surprised by joy, I burst into tears, in gratitude for these people and this place that I have come to love, and for the beneficence of whatever power seems to arrange precious moments such as this.

As I opened the door to the morning, still dark in this autumn season, diamonds of early morning frost shimmered in the grasses. Icy feathery designs covered the windshield of my car. Indescribably beautiful, they glimmered in sparkling silver. Back home, I would have scraped them away with never a notice of their beauty.

Today is an outside task day. I lime the outhouse pit and attach a hasp to the door of the shed. At first touch, my fingers adhere to the metal. I feel the bite of Canadian cold and think of the fishermen, wondering at the number of times that their hands have been frostbitten.

On a late afternoon walk, I climbed the path to the white cliffs. As I looked out on the water and watched a fishing boat disappear over the horizon, I thought of the lives of the people who live here. I am learning some of their stories. Old stories. New stories. Epics of adventure and tales that tug at the heart. All are true, and all involve the sea.

A woman told me of her two sons, each of whom will carry on the fishing trade of their father. A Merchant Marine Captain, who lives in a home overlooking the Bay of Fundy, spoke of a lifetime at sea and described how, after retiring, he would go to a special spot, look out over the ocean, and cry. For folks here the sea runs thick in the blood – compelling, familiar, and dark as the rocks upon which they live.

Late in the day a light breeze came up. As I lay on the porch in meditation, a gust of wind blew in from nowhere and whistled through the screen. I smiled recognition, and drew in deeply.

Tonight on CBC, I am listening to plaintive Celtic music. It has been dark, and now it is raining. If ever an atmosphere were conducive to sadness, this is it.

I have never thought much about my own pain. When my father died, I worked day and night for the next forty-eight hours, cleaning my house from top to bottom. After Emma, I walked for days and days. When I am sad, I keep busy or I get mad – mad at the state of the world, mad at God. Either way, I don't grieve. Up here, away from business and the lure of *busy-ness*, I am face up against raw reality. Today I just let sadness sweep over me. In a play on words, Thoreau would say, "… It was morning, and lo, it is now evening, and nothing memorable is accomplished…"[4] I know better. And so did he.

Day 17

More rain arrived this morning. I lit the candle, and did a long walking meditation as the storm buffeted the Dipper. All of my life I have been headed here.

As the weather broke up, low cloud patches raced by. The moisture in the air kept the wonderful fir and sea smells swirling around as I struck out for a walk to the beach. Today I stood for a long time, forming a visual image of the view out over the shoreline to take back to the States with me.

It has become really clear that I need to discontinue this journal, at least for now. I love to write, and I am glad to have done this during my early time here at the Dipper – before roads are upgraded to tar and the place loses its feeling of seclusion. But the way is closing to writing. Perhaps this is because I am running out of words. More likely – I no longer need to save the Dipper on paper. My experiences and observations are etched into my evolving character – and that is entirely enough.

Day 18

Up early, I ponder my time here and reflect that the only event that could make this final stay of the year more complete would be the sighting of a moose.

I needed to gas up beforehand for my trip home, as I plan to leave very early in the morning. As I drove down the pathway to the street heading out to the convenience store in Lepreau, I turned a somewhat blind corner and came face-on with – guess what? – a moose and her juvenile offspring. She was no more than twenty feet from me. She looked like she was ten feet tall. I felt as if I were driving a matchbox car.

I have seen moose before in the States, but nothing like this. My son Craig worries that, should I hit a moose, it would slide into and through the front windshield. This one would have crushed the roof as the car passed under its stomach. Bunnies, red squirrels, and moose surely grow big in New Brunswick.

Mama moose turned, casually walked ahead of me up the road, and then lumbered off into the woods with her baby. Those yellow roadside signs with a picture of her species and the word "Attention" have now taken on a whole new meaning.

I am out early for one last walk. Half way down the path, I am broadsided by the smell of spruce, as the fragrance of New Brunswick rises up to meet me. I move off the front of my stride and raise my eyes.

By this time, it is late enough in the morning to stop at the farm for a last autumn visit and a travel blessing from Preacher Bill. Whatever happens when he imparts it, it feels good, and it feels right. And today he adds, "Take care of yourself. We need you as a neighbor."

So, here I am, a real hybrid, like the car that I am planning to buy. An almost-Quaker, with a Unitarian connection and a Buddhist practice, getting a travel blessing from a Baptist Preacher.

As I leave the company of Patty and Bill, two folks who, like me, have lived most of their lives during the twentieth century, I ponder the events of these past hundred years. It has been a time of horror, marked by cruel mass demonstrations of man's inhumanity to man, but it also was a time of momentous advancement in the cause of the respect for the personhood of every individual. This occurred as the result of the courageous acts of people with novel ideas. People like Ghandhi. People like King. They both died violently as they were engaged in acts of nonviolence.

Perhaps in the twenty-first century, this cause will be expanded into a new world order, where the beliefs and customs of all individuals are respected, and no person, state, or nation is used for the gain and comfort of another. The twenty-first century belongs to our grandchildren. What a challenge! What an opportunity! Go for it, guys!

I would like to make life easier for those I love – step in and prevent or solve their problems. But that would be like transplanting the pointed firs in order to promote new growth – putting them in my yard, for example. I would like to change the world and make it whole and healthy. But in reality I can only do that for myself. I must remember that acceptance of things as they are is not necessarily capitulation. Rather it has to do with a cessation of railing against life. Sometimes it is the essential act of striving. The leading edge.

I returned to the cabin to begin packing up in earnest. There are some walks that I haven't taken this trip. The trail to the beaver pond. The path behind the cemetery. The trek through the woods to Musquash. I am becoming so much better at leaving things for another time.

If our years on earth can be divided into seasons, I am in early winter. The children are grown. My career is nearing an end. Time is running out, as eventually it does for everything. Here at the Dipper, that arrangement makes sense. But there is still a work to do. It involves surrender. Laying everything down – even this pen. It involves allowing myself to become conscious. To become consciousness itself. To fully enter this life before I depart it. Ahead, I see a cave – a cave of light.

~

I take a final short walk, climbing the far hill. As I look out over the bay, I notice the stump of a dead tree. Inspecting it more closely, I find that it takes the shape of a hand raised in a blessing. Toward me? Toward Dipper Harbour? Toward the sea? No matter. It is what it is.

Time to go. The cottage has been swept, the garbage emptied, the water drained down, the outhouse limed, and the mousetraps set. I will leave early in the morning

Day 19

The wind is slamming the screen door. I open it to the weather. *S-S-S-Swish* . . . the wind blasts through the trees. Rain blows sideways in sheets from west to east. The pond is swept by rapid bands of disturbance, such as the brush stroke of an artist thrown hastily onto paper. As I walk to the car, I step to the wild dance of the pointed firs.

CAPE COD, MASSACHUSETTS

I have news from the Dipper. Darren has put in lots of new trees of all kinds, as well as more flowering bushes and plants, and has even begun clearing a home site for himself. Douglas and Lorri have moved into their year-round home. The Dipper has withstood a siege of carpenter ants, and the red squirrels have yet to succeed in establishing a beachhead in the rafters of the cabin.

Back in Massachusetts, life moves along. Julia is doing beautifully and is a wonderful blessing for our family. Mom gave up her license on her ninetieth birthday. What a difficult transition this is for old people. In a single act, life is completely changed. Paul has a plaque in his office that reads, "Old age is not for sissies." That's for sure.

I am still working and I continue to meditate, albeit with less consistency than when I am in Canada. Shirley, Sue, and I have begun a group meditation practice. It is deeply bonding, and I consider it sacred space. I get to a Quaker meeting as often as I can.

We have had lots of snow on the Cape this year, but winter is beginning to give way to spring, and I am feeling a familiar nudge. I am hostage to a cerebral imprint formed sixty years ago in a small wooded area behind my childhood home. My belongings are packed.

It is time to go.

The road beckons – north.

WORK CITED

[1] Thoreau, Henry David. *Walden*. Princeton, NJ: Princeton University Press, 1989, p. 83.

[2] Ibid., 75.

[3] Ibid., 102.

[4] Ibid., 103.

Suggested Reading

Baylor, Byrd, and Peter Parnall. *The Other Way to Listen*. New York: Alladin Paperbacks, 1978.

Beck, Charlotte Joko. *Nothing Special: Living Zen*. New York: Harper Collins Publishers, 1993.

Bode, Richard. *Beachcombing at Miramar: The Quest for an Authentic Life*. New York: Warner Books, 1996.

Faith and Practice of the New England Yearly Meeting of Friends. A privately published description of Quaker practice adopted at the 1985 New England Yearly Meeting of Friends. A similar, more current version can be purchased at Quaker meetings.

Hines, Sherman. *New Brunswick*. Halifax, Nova Scotia: Nimbus Publishing Limited, 1989.

Johnston, William, ed. *The Cloud of Unknowing and the Book of Privy Counseling: An Enduring Classic of Christian Mystical Experience*. New York: Image Books, 1973.

Kabat-Zinn, Jon. *Wherever You Go, There You Are: Mindfulness Meditation in Everyday Life*. New York: Hyperion, 1994.

Ludlum, David M. *The National Audubon Society Field Guide to Weather*. New York: Alfred A. Knopf, 1991.

Mitchell Stephen, trans. *Tao Te Ching, A New English Version*. New York: HarperCollins, 2000

Spyri, Johanna. *Heidi*. New York: Scholastic Book Services, 1974.

Stoddart, Heidi Jardine. *East to the Sea*. Halifax, Nova Scotia: Nimbus Publishing Limited, 2006.

Thoreau, Henry David. *Walden*. Princeton, NJ: Princeton University Press, 1989.

Whitmire, Catherine. *Plain Living: A Quaker Path to Simplicity*. Notre Dame, Indiana: Sorin Books, 2001.

ABOUT THE AUTHOR

Born in Boston, Massachusetts, in 1938, Marlene Denessen attended Brown University for one semester, leaving at the age of eighteen to marry. Years later, as a single mother of six children, she undertook and completed a Doctoral education while on welfare, supplementing the family finances by waitressing.

Dr. Denessen has worked as a Psychologist for almost thirty years. The grandmother of eleven, she lives on Cape Cod, where she is a Volunteer Naturalist for the Massachusetts Audubon Wildlife Sanctuary. She has traveled extensively by automobile through the western United States and in Maritime Canada in the company of her young adult grandchildren, lodging in a tent and cooking on a tiny camp stove.

Marlene's interests include the history and culture of Native People and the universal spiritual quest. She is especially involved in the cause of the preservation of the environment. In her spare time, she enjoys hiking, reading, and particularly playing her Native American flute. She summers in a tiny camp in the woods of coastal New Brunswick.

Dr. Denessen and her grandson Derrick Soares are co-authors of *Luminous on the Threshold: Hope for the Bereaved and Help for Those Who Would Stand By Them* (Philadelphia: Xlibris Publishing, 2007).